Strategies
& Tactics for the
First Year
Law Student

ASPEN PUBLISHERS

Strategies & Tactics for the First Year Law Student

Maximize Your Grades

By
Kimm Alayne Walton, J.D.
and
Lazar Emanuel, J.D.

With contributions by
Eric S. Lambert, J.D.
and
Alex Ruskell, J.D.
Roger Williams University School of Law

Wolters Kluwer
Law & Business

AUSTIN   BOSTON   CHICAGO   NEW YORK   THE NETHERLANDS

Aspen Publishers
Attn: Permissions Department
76 Ninth Avenue, 7th Floor
New York, NY   10011-5201

To contact Customer Care, e-mail customer.service@aspenpublishers.com, call 1-800-234-1660, fax 1-800-901-9075, or mail correspondence to:

Aspen Publishers
Attn: Order Department
PO Box 990
Frederick, MD 21705

Printed in the United States of America.

1 2 3 4 5 6 7 8 9 0

ISBN 978-07355-9107-3

About Wolters Kluwer Law & Business

Wolters Kluwer Law & Business is a leading provider of research information and workflow solutions in key specialty areas. The strengths of the individual brands of Aspen Publishers, CCH, Kluwer Law International and Loislaw are aligned within Wolters Kluwer Law & Business to provide comprehensive, in-depth solutions and expert-authored content for the legal, professional and education markets.

CCH was founded in 1913 and has served more than four generations of business professionals and their clients. The CCH products in the Wolters Kluwer Law & Business group are highly regarded electronic and print resources for legal, securities, antitrust and trade regulation, government contracting, banking, pension, payroll, employment and labor, and healthcare reimbursement and compliance professionals.

Aspen Publishers is a leading information provider for attorneys, business professionals and law students. Written by preeminent authorities, Aspen products offer analytical and practical information in a range of specialty practice areas from securities law and intellectual property to mergers and acquisitions and pension/benefits. Aspen's trusted legal education resources provide professors and students with high-quality, up-to-date and effective resources for successful instruction and study in all areas of the law.

Kluwer Law International supplies the global business community with comprehensive English-language international legal information. Legal practitioners, corporate counsel and business executives around the world rely on the Kluwer Law International journals, loose-leafs, books and electronic products for authoritative information in many areas of international legal practice.

Loislaw is a premier provider of digitized legal content to small law firm practitioners of various specializations. Loislaw provides attorneys with the ability to quickly and efficiently find the necessary legal information they need, when and where they need it, by facilitating access to primary law as well as state-specific law, records, forms and treatises.

Wolters Kluwer Law & Business, a unit of Wolters Kluwer, is headquartered in New York and Riverwoods, Illinois. Wolters Kluwer is a leading multinational publisher and information services company.

Dedication

This book is dedicated to the hundreds of thousands of students who have wandered through the mazes and labyrinths of first year law, unadorned, unattended, and unassisted.

To the hundreds of thousands who will follow in their path, we offer this little guide in the hope it will help to light the way.

Table of Contents

CHAPTER 1

Introduction

There is no mystery about getting to the top of your law school class. All you have to do is score more points on your exams than your classmates do. It is as simple as that.

This book is designed to teach you how to achieve that goal. Ultimately, any work you do must contribute to that one crucial result: scoring more points on your exams. You will become frustrated if the time you spend studying does not produce results. You would be amazed at how hard some students work without rising from the bottom of the class. Their problem is not that they don't work hard *enough*, but that they work *ineffectively*. If you follow the principles in this book, you will avoid that trap. You will maximize your exam performance while minimizing your study time.

You must master three skills before taking a law school exam. In order to excel, you must be able to

❶ understand the law,

❷ remember the law, and

❸ apply the law to sets of facts.

One reason these skills are difficult to attain is that most professors never actually tell you what you need to do on your exams. Instead, they speak somewhat vaguely about teaching you to "think like a lawyer." They neglect to tell you that what you will be asked to do on your exams is to *apply rules and principles to facts*. Unlike an undergraduate exam, where you basically regurgitate the principles you learned in class, a law school exam is closer to being handed a box of blocks and being told to build a castle. This book will teach you how to convert your class lectures, along with material from your textbooks and secondary sources, into the critical, usable information you will need for your exams. This book will teach you how to predict what your professor will include on her tests. This book will teach you exam skills—the skills that ensure that your performance will reflect your knowledge. And this book will help you create a study schedule that will not keep you chained to a desk until midnight every night. This book will show you what to do, and how and why to do it. These techniques are so effective that you can modify them to suit your own tastes and study habits and still achieve the goals your studying must accomplish.

The Seven-Step Approach to Success on Exams

There are seven basic components to top exam performance:

❶ The Mind-Set of Success
❷ Drawing a Bead on Your Professor
❸ Class Preparation
❹ Taking Notes
❺ Outlining
❻ Test Preparation
❼ Working with Practice Tests

Reading this list, you may worry that you're in for a great deal of work. In fact, if you use the techniques this book outlines, you will obtain the best possible results from the least amount of study time. The secret of the approach is its "telescoping" nature: Once you have performed any task—such as reading a case in your casebook—you will never repeat it. After taking notes in class, you will never rewrite them; instead, you will summarize them, converting them from a class discussion into a usable outline. You will never read anything without thinking about it, summarizing it, and condensing it. By taking an active role in your work, you will reduce your study time and make it more effective, and your exam performance will benefit.

Of course, you *will* have to work to get superior grades, and if you aren't used to doing your homework regularly, you will have to change your habits. (This book will show you how to do this in Chapter 4, Studying and Class Preparation.) If this book told you that you could eat everything you wanted, give up exercising, and still lose weight, you wouldn't believe it. In the same way, if this book told you that you could get terrific grades without working, you would know it was lying. However, if you establish the habit of working effectively, as outlined in this book, studying will become much easier, and you will reach your full potential as a law student. Importantly, *you* are responsible for your own success—no one will do it for you. You need to plan and set yourself up to succeed rather than fail. You also need to take advantage of any help your law school offers (academic support professionals, your professors, etc.). Finally, while as an undergraduate you may have been able to wait until the last minute and still pull it together, that strategy is not going to work in law school (especially in your legal writing courses). Every year, students fall into this trap and spend the rest of law school (perhaps the rest of their legal careers) trying to dig out of it.

Welcome to the beginning of your legal career—good luck!

CHAPTER 2
The Mind-Set of Success

Before you can successfully use the techniques in this book, you must be absolutely convinced that you can and will succeed. If you've started your classes, you may already have begun to doubt your ability to triumph on your exams. This book identifies seven sources that often contribute to this self-doubt: your classmates, your professors, your reading assignments, your personal commitments, your academic background, your unrealistic expectations of yourself, and your unshaken belief that law is too difficult.

This book will address each of these sources of anxiety, but first you should focus on something more basic—why it's so important to believe you can attain superior grades. If you are convinced that you can excel, you will be motivated to overcome obstacles and achieve your goal. With that motivation, you will work to understand and adopt the techniques in this book. Without motivation, you will find ample opportunities and excuses to give up along the way. A positive mind-set is absolutely crucial to your success in law school, as in everything else you do.

Your Classmates

You may believe your classmates are simply more intelligent than you and that no amount of effort will overcome your shortcomings. You can overcome this feeling just by acknowledging the probable source of this belief—the things your classmates say to you. You can't actually see them learning because it's impossible to probe another student's thought processes. You base your belief on what they say about themselves, both in and out of class. In fact, there are a few common problems concerning classmates.

They Sound Really Smart When They Answer in Class

When a student says something intelligent-sounding during class, you may decide that he has some special insight into the law that you lack. But there are several other possibilities, all equally likely.
For example, a person who consistently comes up with the correct answer might have obtained the class notes of someone who has

already taken the class. Professors frequently present the same lectures, using identical notes, year after year. Students with copies of these notes know exactly which hypothetical questions will be asked, and when. Wouldn't you find it easy to sound smart if you knew what questions would be asked and could prepare the answers in advance? Of course you would. Another possibility is that a student might already have found some helpful study materials. Students who read study materials before each new topic comes up in class will know how to resolve the thorny issues because they are better prepared. A third possibility is that the student is simply an extrovert who likes to talk and enjoys using the law school lecture hall as a soapbox—once you start really listening, the student is not so smart after all. Every law school class has a couple of students like this, and they are never as smart as they sound at first. If you ask an upperclass student who the big talkers were during her first year of law school, she will tell you that they were rarely at the top of the class.

These examples should show you that a good answer in class doesn't necessarily mean that the student is smarter than you. Even if it did, remember this book's original premise—the only thing that counts are your exam scores. The person giving a great answer in class may have some special insight that you haven't yet developed, but that doesn't matter. All that matters is that you have that insight when you go into the exam. If you follow the techniques given here, you will understand everything you need to know, and you will be more likely to get top grades than today's class hotshot.

They Claim They Never Study, or They Claim They Study All the Time

Remember, you have no idea how much your classmates actually study; you only know what they tell you. When someone mouths off about his study habits, ask yourself this question: Why is he telling me this? Anyone who tells you about his study habits wants his confession to have an effect on you. The "I-never-study" brag is a popular British prep-school ploy. Think about what this device does—when classmates tell you they never study, you may relax your own efforts. Or you may become anxious, believing that they must understand the material better than you. If they manage to get either reaction, they gain a competitive edge.

Any student who tells you she studies all the time will evoke one of two emotions: sympathy or anxiety. If she tells you she closes the library every night, you will immediately recall the hour you spent playing video games or watching a movie. You will picture this zealot, studying diligently in the library, gaining more points on you with every minute she spends bent over her notes.

This book will soon show you why this reaction is unwarranted. Studies repeatedly indicate that it's not the quantity of study time that counts, but the quality. If a classmate spends all of his time studying, it's more likely that he is studying ineffectively than that he has an edge on you. Students at the bottom of the class work surprisingly hard; they just don't work efficiently. With a sensible study schedule, any student should have time for a life outside of school.

In sum, don't listen when people tell you about their study habits. If you use the techniques in this book, you will develop a study schedule that will maximize your own exam performance no matter what anyone else in your class says or does.

Okay, So They Are Smarter Than You

Assume for a moment that you actually have some classmates who are brighter than you. This should not discourage you because, as in life itself, intelligence is not necessarily a harbinger of success. Poor performance in law school is generally not the result of a lack of intelligence. After all, getting through college and into law school does require some brain power. More common contributors to failure on exams are these: too little time spent studying, chronic and severe problems with test taking, and unexpected life crises. The techniques outlined in this book will combat the first two factors. And, while there is little you can do to prevent a life crisis. If you do find yourself facing one, immediately contact your dean of students and your school's academic support professional—they are there to help you in exactly this kind of emergency.

True, the brighter students may be able to pick up concepts somewhat more quickly than you, *but it doesn't really matter*. Research shows no correlation between how quickly a student understands a concept and how well she remembers it. Even if it takes you a little longer to understand something, you can discipline yourself to remember it just as well as someone who immediately "gets it." Again, the only thing that counts is what you write on your exams. The question,

"How long did it take you to figure this out?" will never appear anywhere. Even if some classmates have higher IQ's than you, you can match or exceed them on exams.

Your Professors

Law school professors are well known for spreading fear among students. Intentionally or unintentionally, they may cause you to think you're not lawyer material. Some of this intimidation is a direct result of the Socratic method, which this book discusses in Chapter 5, Note-Taking and the Classroom Experience. This method can be demoralizing because your professor, who has had years of dedication to her subject, is the one framing all the questions. You can't expect to outsmart her in class. If you simply accept this before she calls on you, you should be able to tolerate the humiliation and inadequacy inherent in her use of the Socratic method.

But there are several other situations that can make you feel small and inadequate. For example, suppose you say something stupid in class. Everyone says stupid things *some* of the time. Don't tell yourself, "Only an idiot would say something like that. I said it, so I must be an idiot, and I can't possibly do well in this course." Instead, you should tell yourself, "Okay, I said something stupid. That doesn't make me a stupid person, and it says nothing at all about my intrinsic worth as a student. I am an intelligent person who simply made a stupid comment under pressure. It doesn't mean I will never respond intelligently again, or that I will do poorly on my exam." If it seems inconceivable that you can change the way you think of yourself by what you tell yourself, keep in mind that what makes you feel inadequate is exactly that—something you tell yourself. You will always be measuring yourself, and you should think thoughts that make you feel better about yourself, not thoughts that discourage you.

Another common source of intimidation is the usual professor's attitude toward study aids. Professors generally fall into two camps when it comes to study aids: There are those who write them (or allow their names to be used on them)—and there are more and more of these all the time—and those who do not. The first camp will typically tell you that study aids are a useful secondary source for studying. Many of the rest refer to study aids contemptuously, insist that they are a form of cheating, or claim that the answers to their exams can't be found in a study aid. You probably already know this to be false.

Your professor may have his own unique way of phrasing or interpreting the rules, but, remember, he can't ignore or reinvent them. While, obviously, your professor is the last word on the law when you deal with his exams, and you must tailor your studies to his approach, there's simply no way for the average student to deny the benefit of reviewing secondary materials. As for the charge of cheating, whom are you cheating when you use a study aid? Your obligation, which you owe only to yourself, is to perform as well as you possibly can, and to do it within the rules. You are under no obligation to make this as difficult as possible for yourself. You will have only one opportunity to perform well on your exams, and what you write on your exams is what counts. If secondary sources increase your self-confidence, give you the exam skills you need to excel, and improve your grades, then to study without them is only cheating yourself.

Ironically, many students find that those professors who are loudest in their attacks on study aids are often those who are the least coherent. Some professors seem to want students to believe that there is something mystical about the law, and that the clouds of mystery will part only through a combination of brilliance, intuition, and grueling work. This is simply untrue. Only a few judges qualify as geniuses, and, if you look carefully at the lawyers you know, and at the upperclass students in your school, you will realize that many of them would not exactly have beaten Einstein in a game of chess. During the first year of law school, you must learn rules, theories, policies, and rationales. You will be asked to apply these to sets of facts, or to draw analogies from them to situations that are presented to you. That's all there is to it, and there's nothing mysterious about it. Your task is to learn the rules, analyze the facts, apply the rules to the facts, and be able to explain what steps you took and why you took them.

If you're still tempted to follow your professor's advice and avoid study aids, then ask yourself: "What if she is wrong? What if I could have done better using study aids?" Will your professor explain to your prospective employers that you did the honorable thing by toughing out your courses without study aids? Will your professor hire or support you? Not very likely. If you use every tool when you need help, you aren't being less prudent or less honorable than those who don't. Don't let anyone intimidate you into ignoring your own best interests.

Finally, you may feel intimidated by the elusive goal of "thinking like a lawyer." Don't worry about it. It's just an abbreviation for a simple series of disciplined steps: (i) learning the basic rules, (ii) reading each case or set of facts carefully, (iii) summarizing the facts and issues, (iv) analyzing (in detail) how to apply the rules to the facts, and (v) subjecting your analysis (or the court's analysis) to critical intellectual review.

If you work at learning and applying these simple steps, before very long, you will hear one of your classmates say that you "think like a lawyer." Very simply, you will have developed the ability to spot the issues, remember the rules, apply the rules to the facts, and draw reasonable conclusions. Your exam scores will reflect this intellectual development.

Your Reading Assignments

If you feel discouraged by your assignments, it's probably because the sheer volume of work can seem overwhelming at first. You may have already decided that you can't possibly master all the material. Here's how to deal with this worry.

Focus on Small, Attainable Goals

If you already feel daunted by the work, it's probably because you're staring at your 1,500-page Criminal Law text, your 1,800-page Property text, and so on. This is a self-defeating way of thinking. Instead, think only about your assignments for today, or, at the most, this week. Put the long-term picture out of your mind and let one small step follow another. Today, you may have to read and summarize only 100 pages, and this is well within your grasp. And if it's too much for today, remember that, as time goes on, you will learn ways to improve your study speed and skills and it will all fall into place. You will also learn to prioritize your work. For example, in addition to your core first-year courses, most law schools require first-year students to enroll in legal writing courses and to participate in a moot court. This book addresses these responsibilities later, but it is important to note here that you should not prioritize your legal writing course or moot court work over your other classes. Simply break up the projects into daily or weekly "assignments" and add them to your list of things to do.

If you have a tendency to worry about all the work that lies ahead, develop the habit of planning each day's work. You should do this through a set weekly schedule, but you should also consider writing it down to make it feel more manageable. Every night, list everything you have to do tomorrow on one side of a sheet of paper (or 3" × 5" card). First, list all your "fixed" activities, such as your class schedule, your appointments, and so on. Then, list all the study assignments you have to complete *that day*. Keep the card with you throughout the day, adding things as you think of them, and crossing things off as you complete them. If, at the end of the day, you haven't completed everything, transfer the items that remain onto the card for the next day. You will find that the habit of pinpointing specific tasks and seeing them on paper makes them seem much more manageable than if you let them float around vaguely in your mind.

Always be sure to note the things you've already done. Every law student has a lot to do every day. But if you stay focused on today's schedule, and on the sequence of things you've finished and still have to do, you will learn to control your time and your fate.

Some Cases in Your Textbook Are Intentionally Confusing

Textbook and casebook authors have an annoying habit of including cases that are confusing or wrong-headed. Their purpose in including these cases is to challenge you to discover why they're wrong, to analyze them carefully, and to spell out a more logical or reasonable conclusion. These cases are often intermingled with cases and notes that are supposed to be teaching you the correct basic principles. It's often difficult to know that a case was wrongly decided before you know the principles that should govern.

Remember that some materials are confusing because they're supposed to be. To help you recognize these, a study aid is particularly valuable. Most study aids contain cases that stand for the correct viewpoint on any issue, as well as clear and concise statements of majority and minority views on all relevant issues. If you use them, you'll recognize when a court has made the wrong decision and you'll spare yourself many minutes of needless analysis. Always bear in mind that efficient use of time is your best ally.

Don't Overburden Yourself

While it's true that law school represents a fresh start after your undergraduate career, don't try to change all your habits at one time. This is not the time to stop smoking, train for a marathon, or lose weight. Law school is demanding, and you should concentrate on your primary goals—understanding and applying the law and getting good grades—and on reducing other stressors, not adding to them. If you take on too much at one time, you are more likely to become anxious and to perform less well in class and on your exams.

Use Available Help

Many students make the mistake of failing to take advantage of the help available at their law schools. Academic support professionals, writing instructors, writing centers, law tutors, and librarians are all ready and willing to help you do your best in law school. While you may never have used available help as an undergraduate, you are making a big mistake if you don't use it in law school. (Remember: You're being evaluated against your fellow students, so you should take advantage of any help your law school offers.) Most importantly, go to any academic support workshops offered by your school. (Most schools offer workshops on many of the issues discussed in this book, including Reading, Note Taking, and Exam Writing.) This small time investment will pay big dividends. Also make sure you take advantage of (and take seriously) any hypothetical or practice exams offered by your professors or the academic support program—the best way to prepare for exams is to practice, and this may be the only feedback you get until you actually sit down for your exams.

Class Web Sites and E-mail

Nowadays, most law classes have a Blackboard or TWEN (The West Education Network) page to provide information to students. Additionally, most communications from your law school's administration will be through e-mail. You will be responsible for any information posted or sent to you. While you may feel like your inbox is inundated every day with 100 messages that don't pertain to you, you can't afford to miss the 101st that tells you the deadline for class registration or the deadline for turning in your legal writing assignment. Make sure you read all of it.

Your First Year Will Not Last Forever

John F. Kennedy once said that he could handle any pain if he knew it was going to end. Hopefully, while you should never have to equate law school with pain, remember the wisdom of another American president, "this, too, shall pass" (Abraham Lincoln). No matter how much work there is each day, one day will follow another until your exams have come and gone. When your final exams are over, that's it—you're done with First Year. If you keep this in mind, it will help you to cope.

Your Personal Commitments

You may have a job, a family, or other major responsibilities that leave you with less time to study than your classmates. Outside pressures can lead you to feel that you will be lucky to pass, let alone excel. Here are some ideas to help you handle these pressures.

Remember that You Are Not Alone

The average age of beginning law students in the United States continues to rise; currently, the average student is in his late twenties. With the rising cost of law school, the number of people who can afford to go through school without working is rapidly diminishing. If you keep in mind that many others are in the same boat, with the same pressures and time constraints, your feelings of helplessness will lessen and your performance will improve.

Having Less Time Can Actually Be an Asset

Interestingly enough, studies show that students with less time available for studying actually waste less time, apply more efficiency to their studies, and achieve better grades. If they have to be well organized, people seem to become more productive.

If you have a number of commitments each day, you simply have to schedule your study time around them. Research has consistently shown that the quality of your studying is more important than the quantity. This book will show you how to use your time effectively. Effective studying, and the use of helpful secondary study aids, will eliminate any competitive disadvantages you might you have.

Your Academic Background

You may be concerned about some things that are part of your past. Here's why these historical factors should not worry you.

Your Performance as an Undergraduate

This cry might sound familiar: "You can't get into law school without being a whiz kid." It's a widely held belief that only the cream of the academic crop is admitted to law school. However, admissions data reveal many law students whose college performance was, at best, mediocre.

If you worked diligently as an undergraduate, you will not be daunted by the process of succeeding in law school. If you did not, however, you may suspect that you're the only slow fish who slipped through the net and that you can't possibly make it. This is sheer nonsense. If you learn to study efficiently, your undergraduate career will have no impact on your law school performance, and you should put it firmly behind you. If you lack good study habits, however, this is the time to develop them, and this book will show you how. Law school does not require an overwhelming amount of work, but if you fall behind, it's very difficult to catch up.

Your Performance on First-Semester Exams

Your fears may be aggravated by a mediocre performance on your first-semester exams. It is extremely common for students to perform poorly on first-semester exams. For most law students, this is the first time during law school that they received any feedback at all on their work (except for Legal Writing courses), and, for many students, these grades might have been the worst grades they have ever received in their academic career. Don't panic or start looking for a new career path—these grades are only a snapshot of what you were able to do within a specific, short time period while answering a specific set of questions. They say nothing about how successful you will be as a lawyer.

Even so, you need to address the problem as soon as you return from winter break. While your poor performance may discourage you, tell yourself that you're going to do better. Take a hard look at what you did during the first semester and make the adjustments necessary for success. Did you start your outlines too late? Did you fail to follow a set study schedule? Did you goof off more than you should have? Did you write your law exams like college essays? Did you know all the black letter law for every class? Remember that many people who excel on first-semester exams actually take a dive on their finals, because they permit themselves to be lulled into a false sense of security and confidence (consequently, you can make up some lost ground in your class rank). A poor performance on your first-semester exams doesn't mean that you're a failure or that you won't succeed on your finals. Repeat to yourself, "I didn't do so well on my first exams, but this doesn't mean I'm stupid or can't become a good lawyer. It has no bearing on how I will perform on the rest of my law school exams. All it means is that, with a little extra work and concentration, I would have done much better."

While it may be painful, you will benefit by analyzing closely what you did wrong on your exams. (In fact, you absolutely should meet with all your professors and your school's academic support professionals to discover *exactly* what you did or didn't do on your first-semester exams. You may think you know what you did wrong without meeting with them, but people are notoriously bad judges of their own work.) Don't stick your head in the sand and simply hope the next round of exams will go better. (Einstein defined insanity as doing the same thing over and over again and expecting different results.) When you review your exams with your professors, you may find that, despite your best intentions and preparations, you panicked and lost your way. Or your thoughts and conclusions were disorganized. Or you missed a critical issue. Or your prof tested issues you had failed to study. Or you left holes in your substantive analyses. Whatever the problems, you can remedy them on your second-semester exams if you identify the errors you made and work hard to avoid them in the future. Write down what you did wrong, concentrate on eliminating the bad thought habits you were able to identify, and tell yourself you will never do those things again. Remember, it's entirely possible to finish the year with great test scores even if you performed disappointingly on your first-semester exams. Some professors don't even give first-semester exams. When they do, first-semester grades normally weigh far less heavily in your overall course grade than do the final exams.

Your Own Unrealistic Expectations of Yourself

It's important to keep a realistic perspective on what law school, and law school exams, really mean. While motivation and effort are crucial elements of success, unrealistic expectations can hurt or even paralyze you. If you use the study techniques in this book, you will perform as well as you possibly can on your exams. You may not be #1 in your class, but there's only one #1. And he has no greater assurance of success in life than you do.

This book repeatedly stresses the importance of what you write on your exam because that's what your professor will be judging you on. Your professor will not be grading you on your value as a person or on your potential as a practicing lawyer. You will be graded only on what is on your exam, and that has important implications for your measure of yourself. If you have done your very best, your grade will reflect only your performance on this one exam. It doesn't determine whether you're a good and decent person, or even whether you will be a good lawyer. Poor performance does not mean that going to law school was a mistake, that you'll never get a job, or that you'll be subsisting on dog food for the rest of your days. Many excellent lawyers did not perform well in law school. Perhaps the only effect of a less-than-brilliant performance in the first year of law school is to hinder you in obtaining a clerkship at a prestigious law firm after your second year, or to keep you from being on Law Review. Try to keep a realistic perspective on both your abilities and your goals. Don't let yourself get "psyched" out. Most importantly, try to ignore all the law school chatter and static—about grades, jobs, hours, prestige, and so on. Admittedly, it's easier said than done, but you'll be happier if you keep reminding yourself who you are and why you came to law school.

The Fiction that Law School Is Difficult

Many students are impressed at the outset by the notion that law school is a grueling experience. After all, it's comforting to think that you're one of the very few who can wend their way through academia's most treacherous obstacle course. In reality, many students actually enjoy the mental skirmishing the law requires. But few students will admit this, or admit to liking law school, because it's simply not chic to like it. The law is supposed to be difficult. Almost everyone believes this. People who don't attend law school certainly believe it because lawyers tell them how hard it is. In fact, when you come right down to it, if you strip away all the myths, the professorial and judicial mumbo-jumbo, and the pomp, you'll find that law is really not terribly difficult after all.

Learning the law consists primarily of drawing rules from cases, understanding the reasons for the rules, and developing the ability to apply those rules to similar cases. In one form or another, this is what your exams test. An "easy" exam will test these skills at their most basic level. A more difficult exam may ask you to apply an existing rule to make sense of a previously unsettled area, or to balance two rules that seem contradictory. Even in the most difficult examples, you draw analogies to a given pattern of facts from two or more patterns you're familiar with from reading the cases, and then you explain why your analogies should apply. Armed with rules, rationales, and policies that you have applied many times to similar fact patterns, you will find the whole thought process stimulating and rewarding.

Why, then, do so many people consider law so difficult? For one thing, it's human nature to characterize what you do as hard. If you view your activities as difficult, and if you can convince others that this is true, you make yourself seem like a more valuable and important person. After all, you're demonstrating that you can do work that puts you a couple of cuts above the rest of the world. This can be very effective in extracting admiration and sympathy from family and friends. But there is also a trap in overstating the difficulty of your work: You may convince yourself that the study of law is more difficult than it really is. You will tell yourself, "This work is so hard I can't really be expected to do it." These thoughts are debilitating and destructive.

Law school seems excessively difficult because of the way it's taught. The skills you use in class are not the ones you will need to apply on your exams. Imagine yourself as a child again, studying arithmetic for the first time. Suppose you spent an entire year learning the shape and history of Arabic numbers—you traced your finger again and again over sandpaper numbers, you wrote them time after time, and you spent hours studying how each number got its shape. If on your final exam your teacher asked you, "How much are 7 and 4?" You wouldn't have a clue. Obviously, your classroom work and study would not have equipped you to deal with the exam.

Law school is not very different. For a typical class, you will brief and discuss cases decided in English or American courts. In each case, the court will have clearly stated and defined the issues. Your classroom discussion will generally be limited to these issues. But on your exams, you will be given a hypothetical set of facts. Drawing from the issues you've discussed, you will have to identify for yourself the issues that relate to these facts, spell out the rules that apply to each issue, and analyze how those rules apply to the facts. For certain exams, the skills you need may be somewhat different from these, but typically they are not the skills you will have practiced in class. The reality is that you have to learn and practice the skills you need without help from your profs, your casebooks, or your texts. Your school's academic support program will try to teach you these skills. This book will also help. When exam time comes, you won't be alarmed by the format or the content. You will know exactly what to do.

One thing that makes law school more difficult than it needs to be is that law school texts are often confusing. Unlike a college textbook, law school texts are made up of primary sources, namely cases, that are edited for length, not for understanding. Instead of clearing up the confusion, a text will even state that you are not yet expected to understand what it means. By now, you may have heard the old axiom, "Don't worry. Everything in Civ Pro comes together at Spring Break." Does this mean that it is perfectly okay for you to spend all but the last month of your first year in total confusion? Any competent educator will tell you that doesn't make sense. Civ Pro is a long, convoluted, difficult course in which nothing you've ever learned before has any relevance. Your knowledge of the course has to be built step by step, stone by stone, until the whole structure comes together. You have to stop after every new step and make sure you've digested it. You should not accept the notion that there is material you are not supposed to understand. You have it in your power to understand it all just as well as the next person. Just go out and work at it.

Many things are really difficult: Mapping the human genome is difficult; overcoming the AIDS virus is difficult; bringing peace to the world is difficult. Law is not difficult. Remember, law is only a process for controlling the conduct of human beings. It's a system based on experience and reason. You can learn to master it. Hundreds of thousands have before you.

Figuring Out Your Learning Style

If you don't already know how you learn best, you might benefit from figuring out your learning style (usually broken into visual, auditory, read/writing, or kinesthetic). To discover your learning style, you can complete a questionnaire, which is available at www.vark-learn.com. If you are an auditory learner, you may find podcasts or CDs helpful. If you are a visual learner, you may benefit by turning your class outline into a flowchart.

Maintaining the Mind-Set of Success

As President Franklin Delano Roosevelt said, "the only thing [you] have to fear is fear itself"; the only thing that will beat you is your own conviction that you won't make it. Nonetheless, despite your best intentions, you'll sometimes find the pressure getting the best of you. Here are some tips for dealing with this.

Smile

Yes, smile. Laugh out loud. If you force yourself to smile, you will find that this alone will help you put your priorities in perspective.

If this seems ridiculous, try it the next time you are upset—smile your biggest smile. And sing your favorite song. You will be amazed at how effective these remedies can be.

Maintain Your Sense of Self-Worth

No matter what happens to you, it does not reflect on your value as a human being. Developing and maintaining a positive personality is the cornerstone of success. It's not a sign of failure if, at times, you disappoint yourself, or if you pass or say "not prepared" when you're called on in class, or if you fail to reach a specific goal that you set for yourself. If you read the biography of any successful person, you will find that she overcame many more obstacles and missteps than you are ever likely to face. For instance, Thomas Edison claimed to have failed 10,000 times before he successfully produced a working electric light bulb.

Law School Can Feel Like Fourth Grade

Many first-year students complain that the social scene of law school sometimes feels like they've gone back to fourth grade. (Don't worry, this more or less dies out by your second year.) Under the intense pressure of law school, where people are continually comparing themselves to one another and where you see the same people every day and do the exact same things they do, law classes often divide into cliques, rumors start to spread, hearts are won and broken, nicknames are bestowed, and rivalries are begun. Realize that all of this is simply a natural reaction to stress (similar to what happens in boot camp). It's happening in every law school in the nation—not just yours. If possible, ignore it. And if you can't, try to see the humor in it. Don't let it affect how you feel about yourself.

Significant Others Outside of Law School

If you have a significant other who is not in law school with you, be mindful of that fact. You'll need to study a lot, so make time for them. Be with them, rather than at a bar telling in-jokes back and forth with your law friends or, with your newly learned lawyer skills, tearing apart your significant other's desire to go out for Italian food. Your first year of law school will likely be stressful on any relationship you have, so be careful. Otherwise, you might lose it.

Practice Relaxation Techniques

If you find yourself beginning to panic, take a minute to relax. Any diversion will force you to take your mind away from your worries. A good book on meditation will give you detailed advice on relaxation techniques, but there are a couple of simple things you can do yourself: Tell yourself to calm down. Lie down or sit comfortably; close your eyes and concentrate on breathing in and out. Allow your thoughts to come and go aimlessly in your mind; don't let yourself focus on any one thought. Instead, concentrate on, for instance, your hand. Open and close your fingers in slow motion, concentrating only on watching your fingers. Do this for several minutes. You'll find that when you return your focus to the tasks that caused your anxiety, you'll be calmer and better able to handle them.

CHAPTER 3
Drawing a Bead on Your Professor

Throughout your first year of law school—in every year, in fact—you must get inside the mind of each professor to ensure top grades on your finals. This chapter presents tips on how to read your professor. These basic tips will be expanded on throughout the book.

Determining a Professor's Personality Profile and How This Information Will Help You

Remember: You will write your exam answers for an audience of one—*your professor.*

People tend to look favorably on those who agree with them. This tendency is likely to be particularly pronounced with your law professors. Since they've spent a great deal of time thinking about the subjects they teach, it's only natural for them to believe that anyone else who devoted intelligent thought to the same material should come to the same conclusions they have; thus, it's important for you to discover what these conclusions are. Once you've determined where your professor stands, you can use that knowledge to your advantage. On your exam, whenever possible, you should try to reach the same conclusion that your professor would have reached.

You can accomplish this only if you've formulated an accurate picture of her views. Listen carefully to the comments your professor makes in class and to the positions she takes in discussions with students. You should be able to discover fairly quickly whether she is a liberal or a conservative, whether she is plaintiff-oriented or defendant-oriented, whether she emphasizes the dissents in cases or ignores them, and so forth. Record your professor's views in your class notes.

One method is to use your professor's initials, indicating, for example, that "JF disagrees with the decision in this case," or "JF believes this is the better view." Then, on your exam, echo these positions whenever possible. For example, you may discover that your professor is plaintiff-oriented. Knowing this, if you encounter an exam question that asks whether or not a set of facts constitutes a tort, and the facts don't clearly indicate that no tort exists, you should probably conclude that one does, since that's the conclusion a plaintiff-oriented professor would reach.

Similarly, if an exam deals with an area of law in which two authorities or theories conflict—for example, comparative versus contributory negligence—discuss first the one your professor doesn't favor; follow that discussion with a statement such as, "but the better view is . . . ," and then address the one he does prefer. This is a well-known, successful sales technique. A salesperson often proposes two possible courses of action, mentioning last the one he wants the customer to take. It is a psychological fact that a person is most likely to prefer the last option she is given.

Watch for Physical Cues that Reveal What a Professor Believes to Be Important

Your professor is likely to test you on concepts he believes to be the most important; therefore, you need to be able to identify those concepts. In Chapter 5, Note-Taking and the Classroom Experience, this book discusses how your professor, without realizing it, gives you physical cues that reveal what he finds particularly crucial (and thus is likely to be on your exam).

Read Any Publications Your Professor Has Written Concerning the Subject Matter of the Course

Reading what your professor has written is one of the best ways to become familiar with your professor's views. Read any law review articles by your professor that relate to the subject matter of the course you're taking, regardless of whether or not your professor mentions them during class. If your professor distributes any of her articles in class, read them, taking some notes to include in your outline. Do this even if your professor tells you that the article is only supplemental reading. If your professor does not hand out any articles she wrote, find them. Check the index to legal periodicals in the library and your law school's catalog, which probably summarizes your professor's publications. You can even check with your professor's administrative assistant.

You will draw two main benefits from reading your professor's publications. First, the articles will help you to expand on the "personality profile" you're building of your professor.

(Note, though, that if an article was written some time ago, your professor's views may have changed since it appeared.) Second, since topics that interest your professor are the ones most likely to be on his exams, reading the articles (which reveal what he finds especially intriguing) may help you predict what will be tested.

Talk with Second or Third Years Who Have Already Taken This Class with Your Professor

Second and third years love giving advice to first-year students, and you can use this to your advantage. Be sure, though, that your questions are very specific; generalities will not be useful.

When an another student offers you advice, be sure to ask how well he did in your professor's class. If he did well, his advice as to preparation will be very valuable. If he did not do well, he can still be helpful. Ask him what he might have done differently to improve his performance.

It's the Professor's Views that Count

If you hold strong views, you may, at times, find yourself disagreeing violently with your professor, especially if she is also strong-minded. That is perfectly acceptable. Remember, though, that strong convictions, while admirable outside the classroom, may work against you. On the exam, it's the professor's views that count.

During an Exam, Put Your Own Views Aside

On an exam, you may encounter questions that deal with controversial issues. If, for example, a question appears about the merits of the death penalty, or restrictions on abortion, or about the good-faith exception to the exclusionary rule—and you tend to be liberal but know that your professor is very conservative—you must restrain yourself. Resist the urge to spout off about the issue. You won't convert your professor, and you may harm yourself. Think of your restraint not as "selling out" but as a good test of your professionalism. Ultimately, when you practice law, you'll find yourself in situations where you disagree with the views of your clients. Professional behavior requires that you keep your own feelings in check.

When a Professor Disagrees with an Accepted View, Follow Your Professor

Occasionally, you may find that your professor states a principle of law differently from any other source you can find. Remember that your professor is always right. "Right" in this instance means "right" only for the purposes of your exam, and the exam is your primary concern. Think of your class as a kingdom with an absolute monarch. If your professor tells you that murder is "a killing committed with intent," then accept that as the rule, even if you know for a fact that he is wrong. He is, after all, the monarch, and to succeed on his exam, you will have to obey his decree. You don't have to agree with your professor, but you must accept that, in his class, he has the final word. If you find it less confusing, you can actually cross out any statements to the contrary in your study aids and write in the margin what your professor thinks (while carefully noting that these are his opinions).

Getting the Most from Old Exams

Reviewing old exams is standard procedure for any diligent law student. At many law schools, the law library keeps professors' exams on file; sometimes, professors even provide model answers. If you don't use these materials carefully, however, they may do you more harm than good. The following are guidelines to using old exams to your greatest possible advantage.

Make Photocopies of Old Exams as Early in the Semester as Possible

At this point, you may want to put this book down and go to the library to copy old exams. There is a practical reason for this: As exam time approaches, it may become an impossible task. Near the end of the semester, old exams will be signed out of the library almost all the time because everyone will want to use them. Make copies early in the semester to avoid the pre-exam rush.

Don't Look at Old Exams Until You Begin Test Preparation, Late in the Semester

Again, there is a practical reason for this: Looking at old exams before you have a substantial part of the course under your belt can be terribly intimidating. Early in the semester, when you haven't covered much of what will appear on an exam, you'll become discouraged if you read an exam that covers the entire course. Your belief in your ability to succeed on exams is crucial; looking at old tests before you have the knowledge to tackle them can deflate your self-confidence, so it's better not to do it too early.

When you're ready to begin preparing for exams, start by reading Chapter 8, Test-Taking, in this book. Then use old exams to practice. Rather than attempting, at first, to complete an entire practice exam, you may want to tackle only one question at each sitting. Also, don't burden yourself with rigid time constraints when you begin to practice; initially, it's more important to master the skill of test-taking than to time yourself. After sharpening your exam skills, you can begin to time yourself more strictly. Ultimately, the ability to work quickly on exams will be an important ingredient to your success.

In addition to using old exams for practice, you should dissect them. Make note of which topics are covered, as well as how your professor approached them. You will want to know not only what topics your professor favors, but also whether her exams are complex and issue-laden or simple and analytical. Note, as well, whether the exams consist largely of essay questions or of multiple-choice/true-false questions. You should also determine how the topics on the exams correlate with what was covered in class. For example, if your professor rushed through material toward the end of the semester, check to see if she emphasizes it on the exam to make up for the lack of class discussion.

If your professor has provided any model answers to her exams, review them. They will give you great insight into how to write answers on your own exam. Note, for instance, the style and approach of the model answers: Are they presented in a straightforward **I-R-A-C** (**i**ssue, **r**ule, **a**nalysis, and **c**onclusion) format? (A vast majority of model answers follow I-R-A-C format.) Or is your professor one of the few who prefer a rambling, stream-of-consciousness essay on legal theories? Add this information to the "personality profile" of your professor.

CHAPTER 4
Studying and Class Preparation

In this section, you will learn how to maximize the effectiveness of your studying. It covers everything from reading, highlighting, and briefing cases, to methods of scheduling your study sessions in order to achieve the best results.

How Effective Studying and Class Preparation Lead to More Points on Exams

Consistent Preparation Reduces Anxiety

Anxiety interferes directly with performance on exams. Research shows that repetitive studying is the best remedy for test anxiety.

Preparing for Class Enables You to Get Maximum Results from a Professor's Presentation

If you don't prepare for every class by reading and briefing cases, it will be difficult for you to follow what's going on in the classroom. Your experience will be analogous to watching a baseball game without prior knowledge of how the game is played; you'll get very little from the experience. Furthermore, a lack of preparation may divert your attention from absorbing the material to worrying about being called on. On the few occasions when you simply cannot prepare, it's better to tell the professor before class and attend the lecture anyway than to avoid class altogether.

Studying Before a Class Is the First Step Toward Memorizing the Material

The simple truth is, you can't memorize what you don't study. In fact, what most people call "forgetting" is not forgetting at all, but failing to have paid attention in the first place. Remember, your studying and class preparation represent the first, and probably the most focused, contact you will have with the material.

The Basics of Effective Studying

The effectiveness of your studying is determined largely by how active a role you take. Reading is a passive learning activity, so it should comprise no more than half your study time because a more active approach will help you more. For example, if you have two hours available to cover an assignment, and you can read the assignment in half an hour, the least effective way to study would be to read the assignment four times. Instead, read it only twice, following the method described below. Spend the remaining hour asking yourself questions and briefing the relevant cases. Reread only when necessary to clarify points you're unsure of. Spend the time you save to synthesize new materials, relating them to each other and to materials previously covered. You'll probably be tempted simply to read materials again and again; after all, it's far easier to let your eyes meander down a page while your mind wanders than to work, recalling and integrating the material. Don't give in to this temptation. Research supports the importance of incorporating a questioning process into your studying; students who do so average several points higher on tests than students who do not.

An ideal study system forces you to think about what you've read and to make sense of it. The system you should use is a classic one, which this book tailors to the study of law. Five elements make this system work:

❶ it uses strategies that make learning effective (such as making the material interesting and meaningful),

❷ it helps the student identify and understand important points in the material,

❸ it helps the student to remember those points,

❹ it's more efficient than reading the material several times, and

❺ it's easy to learn.

SQ3R

The study system is called "SQ3R," which stands for survey, question, read, recite, and review.

Survey

"Surveying" means getting an overview of what you're about to study before you actually study it. The casebook method of teaching law makes "surveying" harder; it's difficult, if not impossible, to "skim" a case. You can, however, survey each topic before you begin to cover it. Keep an eye on the syllabus so you'll know when a new topic is coming up, and try to familiarize yourself with the topic before it's discussed in class. Even a small amount of familiarity will substantially improve your understanding of material and help you retain the new information.

Some students have found that using a study aid when they begin a new topic makes reading assignments easier to understand and makes class time more productive. Each time you're about to begin a new topic in class, you can look at the information on that topic and run through the material in order to familiarize yourself with the subject. Research confirms that the more you already know about a particular subject the easier it is to absorb new information about it—to understand it and to retain it. With this little head start, you can make the text and classroom material more meaningful, more interesting, and easier to remember.

Question

If you question the material as you read it, you'll find it easier to stay focused and remain interested. Questioning the material forces you to take an active role in learning it: Why is a particular case included? What new issues does it introduce? Asking yourself questions as you read greatly enhances the effectiveness of your study and should add points to your exam scores. This book further discusses the importance of questioning in Chapter 5, Note-Taking and the Classroom Experience.

Read Actively

Read Actively Rather than Passively

Taking an active role in reading cases will shorten your study time later. It will also dramatically improve your ability to understand and memorize material. As described above in the section on surveying, you should have covered the general topic before you began your reading. Now, as you begin to read, ask yourself, "Why is this case here? What does it add to the material on this topic?" You should find that each case will do one of three things:

❶ *announce* a new rule of law,
❷ *modify* a rule of law you've already learned, or
❸ *show that a rule was applied incorrectly.*

As discussed above, questioning the meaning and purpose of a case as you read it will help you focus and, ultimately, will improve your understanding, enabling you to see how the individual details fit into the big picture. Questioning will keep you from missing the forest for the trees.

"How Many Times Should I Read a Case?"

"Oh, no," you're thinking. "They're going to make me read cases over and over. That never helps; I just get bored." With this study system, you won't get bored. You'll read each case only twice, each time with a different purpose.

First Reading: Don't Highlight

The first time you read a case, don't highlight or outline anything. Instead, as you read, ask yourself the questions discussed earlier: "Why is this here? What am I supposed to learn from this case that I didn't learn from the previous one? How does this case relate to others I've read?" On your first reading, try to keep a balanced, broad perspective; don't get lost in the details or try to follow all the permutations. Many cases involve more than one issue. The casebook author may not have edited out portions of the opinion that are extraneous to the issue you're studying. You won't be able to identify the correct issue unless you ask yourself how the case relates to the material you're supposed to be studying.

Why shouldn't you highlight when you read a case for the first time? There are two reasons: First, until you've read the entire case, you won't know what's really important. Because highlighting is so easy to do, most students tend to highlight too much instead of marking only what is important. Second, highlighting on your first run through the material can actually interfere with learning it. Stopping to highlight will interfere with the smooth flow of your reading. Moreover, it's easy to develop the very dangerous habit of highlighting material instead of actually reading it. It's possible to highlight a sentence and move on without ever actually reading the sentence. Ironically, you could end up merely glossing over the most important parts of a case, while actually marking and reading only what's unimportant! If you simply cannot read a case without marking the book somehow, use a pencil only to put a checkmark or a dot next to any line you think important.

Second Reading: Underline or Highlight Key Points

After you've read a case through once, stop and think about it. What were the important points? You should be able to answer the questions that occurred to you while reading, relating this case to other cases you have studied. Now is the time to go back and underline only the key phrases. You need to figure out what the most important sentence of the case is— what sentence, more than any other, states the rule, modification, or mistake that the case stands for in the context of your class.

What if I Don't Understand a Case?

Depending on which casebook you're using, you may occasionally come across cases so confusing that they may as well be printed in another language: The facts make no sense to you, you have no idea what the issue is, and the case seems to go on and on without giving you a shred of meaningful material.

When this happens, you may feel an urge to panic; these cases tend to be very long, so the more you read, the more overwhelmed you feel. This is, without a doubt, a horrible experience, particularly if you convince yourself that, "Everyone understands this material but me. I'm a failure." You're wrong. You are almost certainly not the only one who doesn't understand it, you are certainly not a failure, and there are several things you can do to regain a feeling of control.

Resign Yourself to Not Understanding It

If you've given a case your best effort, and you still don't understand it, perhaps you weren't meant to. A case that appears near the beginning of many Civil Procedure casebooks, *Sibbach v. Wilson*, 312 U.S. 1 (1941), is completely incomprehensible to the vast majority of students. It's a tough case that turns on a very obtuse concept. What makes *Sibbach v. Wilson* even more unfair is that it turns on an issue that's virtually impossible to test, so you probably won't even have to deal with it on your exam. There aren't many situations like this, though, so if you do come across such a case, it might be best simply to concede that you just don't get it. Do your best, move on, and gain whatever understanding you can from some other source, such as classroom discussion, or, again, a good commercial outline or other study aid.

Turn to a Commercial Outline

Because of the importance of taking an active role in learning, you will readily understand why you shouldn't turn to a "canned brief" before you've given a case your best shot. After putting in your best effort, though, it's certainly better to understand a case by reading about it in a commercial outline than to remain in a state of confusion. Most outlines include a discussion of major cases, which makes the cases understandable. Take a look at the various outlines offered by your law school bookstore and talk to other students about what outlines they use. Additionally, your school's academic support office or library may have commercial outlines or other study aids available for your use. Your school's academic support professional is a great resource for discovering what study aids might work best for you.

Recital (Briefing Your Cases)

Briefing gets a bad name in law school. You may consider it a laborious waste of time, and you probably won't have to brief cases formally in your second and third years of law school. Remember, though, that you aren't yet a second- or third-year student. At this point in your law school career, there are two reasons why you should brief cases.

If You're Called on in Class for a Case You Haven't Briefed, Your Professor Is More Likely to Humiliate You

For many people, this is encouragement enough. Because many professors use the Socratic method, humiliation in class is sometimes unavoidable, no matter how well prepared you are; however, your experience will be even more painful if you're poorly prepared. Briefing is the best way to prepare.

Briefing Cases Is a Critical Part of Taking an Active Role in Learning

You can't brief a case without paying careful attention to it and dissecting it. This analysis can be more important to your studying than reading the case in the first place.

How to Brief

You may have learned how to brief cases during your orientation week at law school or in your Legal Writing course. Although individual formats differ, briefing almost always requires that you summarize the facts, the issue, the holding, the rules of law, and the rationale of a case. There are several things to keep in mind.

The Facts Will Be Presented in Greater Detail in Your Brief Than in Your Outline

In order to perform well in class, you must be very familiar with the facts of each case; the facts you list in your brief must "cue" your memory to recall every important fact of a case. Later on, if you decide to include the case in your course outline, you'll need only the "TV Guide" facts: that is, bare-bones information of the sort you read in *TV Guide*. In your outline, you'll include only those facts that have a bearing on the rule the case establishes—the "material" facts, and no others.

A Brief Should Summarize, Not Duplicate

Sometimes, especially if you're rushed, you'll be tempted to copy statements from the case directly into your brief. Try not to do this. Passive transcription of sentences doesn't force you to think about the case and so does not help you absorb information. Instead, try to summarize the case in your own words. (Of course, any rule or definition can and should be copied verbatim.) Copy passages only when you have no time to do anything else, and be sure that you understand the duplicated passages. Don't copy passages just to avoid thinking about them. Don't "book brief" a case—that is, identify the holding, rule, and so on only in the margins of your text—at least, not until you've mastered the art of the full brief. Briefing cases takes time, but it pays off on exams.

Make a Note of the Dissent

If the dissenting opinion of a case is included in your casebook, note its main points; it's there for a purpose. You may find the dissent particularly useful for providing arguments that support the other side of an issue on your exam. Additionally, dissents are often clearer than the majority opinion in discussing the legal issues presented by the case.

A Note on Statutes and Administrative Regulations

Law school may be the first time you have been introduced to the text of statutes and administrative rules and regulations. Just as you have to learn to brief cases, you will have to learn to parse statutes and analyze administrative rules. The following are a few suggestions.

Don't Just Recopy the Statute into Your Notes

It is tempting to simply retype the statute word for word, but it is important that you understand what the statute seeks to accomplish, the rationale behind it, and the consequences of violating it. Put keywords of the statute into your notes and then rephrase it into your own words.

Parsing a Statute

To parse a statute means to break it up into several components and study each component separately. This is the most effective way to understand the statute as a whole. Break the statute into pieces that are easy for you to understand; for example, you might note what persons the statute affects, how it affects them, why it was passed, and the consequences to violators. Then you can merge your class notes, any secondary source material, and related cases with your "parsed" notes.

Understanding Administrative Rules and Regulations

Administrative rules and regulations should be read in a similar manner to statutes. It is important to note which agency passed the regulation and why, as well as how it affects the cases involving it. Always keep in mind the surrounding material in your casebook when you are first introduced to a statute or administrative regulation, because that will help you to understand the rule's applicability.

More About Briefing

Briefing cases is one of the most important tasks you'll do during your first year of law school. You may not realize that briefing cases teaches you an essential skill: the ability to extract the important and relevant elements from a case. Briefing a case and then seeing in class how it compares to the analysis done by your professor and classmates also allows you to compare, evaluate, and adjust your analytical skills.

Every case contains statements, observations, and remarks that are extraneous to the holding of the case; together these are called *dicta*. Only the holding of a case should be relied on as precedent; if you mistakenly rely on *dicta*, you'll be in serious trouble.

Many professors who teach by the Socratic method will expect you to read from your brief during class (see the section, "The Socratic Method," in Chapter 5, Note-Taking and the Classroom Experience). In fact, many of them will be very upset if you try to answer questions about an assigned case from memory. Think about it from their point of view—the class discussion will move more smoothly, and the professor will be better able to discuss the points he wishes, if the student who is called on can interact intelligently with the professor about the case at issue. Requiring a written brief is the one way a professor can make sure that his students have read, digested, and analyzed the case and can discuss it intelligently in class.

Some of your classmates will give up on writing full briefs right away. There's a certain appeal to not briefing; writing a brief for every case is a time-consuming process, increasing the amount of study time you need to spend per subject. However, the best advice is to *write a full brief for each case until you learn to look at a case and pull out all the important elements easily and quickly; once you can do that, you can limit yourself to book briefs.*

Preparing an Effective Written Case Brief

Before briefing any case, you should *read it carefully from beginning to end.* Don't brief as you read! If you do, you'll miss facts and issues that become important as you read through the case. As you brief more and more cases, you may be able to brief the case as you read. This is the skill you're trying to build. It takes time and training and can't be hurried.

It's essential to *write concisely and crisply.* Many students suffer from "lawyer-ese"—they think that the best way to think and sound like a lawyer is to use as many multi-syllable words as they can. (Many law students try to impress their classmates and professors by dropping Latin phrases into their written assignments and even into their everyday conversation!) Both professors and judges like concise and crisp language. There's no need to be long-winded or wordy. Resist the urge.

Once you've read through the case, go back and start your brief. There's a definite structure to a written brief; to guide you, there is a sample template for a brief at the back of this book. It's not the only form you can use, but it works well in practice. You might be asked to write a brief and turn it in as one of your first Legal Writing assignments; in that case, use the form specified by your professor.

Your brief should contain these essential elements:

Case Information

The first thing to do when briefing a case is to identify the parties and the court. Who are the plaintiffs? The defendants? Necessary third parties? What court heard the case? Cases often involve multiple parties, and if you don't understand the parties and the issues, you'll be very embarrassed in class if your professor asks you, "So who won *Jones v. Smith*?" and you don't know the answer.

Why Is This Case Here?

This is probably the most overlooked, but most important, part of the brief. Your job is to fit the case into the "big picture."

Is this a landmark case? A case included for its historical value? An example of a bad decision? A statement of the majority view? The minority view? Is the case here because the *dissent* states an important view of the law? If you include a section in your brief explaining *why* this case is in your casebook, you will slowly develop a better sense of the relationship of one case to another and of the overall organization of the entire subject. (If you're not immediately sure how the case fits in or what it stands for, leave this section blank and come back to it when you have the answers.)

Fact Pattern (Substantive History)

This is a difficult part of the brief to write. The version of the case that appears in your casebook has been *edited down* from the original version. In real life, most cases deal with more than one issue. Because your casebook editor is interested in citing the case for a specific issue that ties the case to other cases on the subject, she will have edited out those sections of the original opinion that do not pertain to the issue being presented. Also, many judges love to write unnecessarily long and wordy opinions to flaunt their scholarship and erudition. Sometimes, therefore, the version that is printed in your casebook will contain many facts *not relevant to the holding of the case.*

Many instructors will tell you that the best way to brief a case is to write the facts first. This is bad advice. It saves a lot of time and effort to *determine what the issues in the case are first* and then reconstruct the facts of the case in the light of the issues you've spotted. All facts related in any way to one of the issues should be included in your statement of facts. All others should be ignored.

Additionally, you should come up with a *keyword or keywords* for each case. For instance, the torts case of *Garratt v. Dailey* involved a boy who pulled the chair out from under someone, causing that person injury. The keywords for this case might be "boy pulls chair." The keywords will help you remember the other facts of *Garratt* when you take your final exam; this, in turn, may help you to see an association between the *Garratt* case and a question on the exam.

Procedural History

The procedural background of a case is often just as important as the substantive background. An appellate court can rule only on those issues brought before it on appeal. It cannot rule on an issue that has not been raised by the parties. (If it does, its decision will be labeled an "advisory opinion," and it will be unenforceable.) A lower court, on the other hand, will decide a case for the first time, and it can make any ruling supported by the facts. You should be sure that your brief describes how the case got to this court, what issues are before the court, what the court is empowered to decide, and what disposition the court has made of the issues.

In the above-cited example, *Garratt v. Dailey*, the trial court had found for the defendant, and the plaintiff appealed. The appellate court (the court that decided the case in the casebook) remanded the case to the trial court for clarification based on the rule of law stated by the court (see below).

Rule of the Case

Every case you read in law school illustrates a specific rule of law. For instance, *Garratt v. Dailey* centers on the principle that "if an actor knows with substantial certainty that an act or occurrence will bring about a desired result, such act or occurrence is intentional." One of the hardest tasks in briefing a case is to determine and state the correct *rule of law* for that case. The rule must be neither too vague nor too specific to the facts of that case. For instance, if you stated the rule as "knowledge with substantial certainty is required for an intentional act," your statement would be too vague; it doesn't show that the knowledge required is knowledge that the act will bring about a desired result. On the other hand, if you stated the rule as "a person who pulls a chair out from under someone has committed an intentional act if he knew with substantial certainty that pulling the chair out would result in harmful or offensive contact," your statement would be too specific and ostensibly limited to the facts cited; the principle involved—that "knowledge with substantial certainty" that an act committed by the actor will bring about a desired result makes the act an intentional act—has a more general application to acts in general and not just the act of pulling out a chair.

You should state the applicable rule of law in your brief twice—first in the issue-by-issue analysis of the case (see below) and again in a section called "concise statement of rule of law." Why write it twice? The rule of law is the most important part of the case, and the one element you have to remember and carry with you. If you remember nothing else, you will at least have the one tool you need most in analyzing the facts and issues in your exam questions.

Analysis of the Issue—Using the I-R-A-C Formula

You've identified the parties, stated the facts, and defined the rule of law of the case. The next step—the core of the brief—is the issue-by-issue analysis. The analysis should be patterned after the I-R-A-C style of answering essay questions. (This stands for **i**ssue, **r**ule of law, **a**pplication of rule to facts, and **c**onclusion. The I-R-A-C method will be discussed in more detail later in Chapter 8, Test-Taking.) You should practice applying the I-R-A-C model wherever possible; this helps you prepare for your exams. Don't be confused if your Legal Writing courses use a different acronym. Depending on style and what your Legal Writing professor chooses to emphasize, this basic formula is sometimes denoted in several different ways, including C-R-A-C, T-R-R-A-C, or I-R-R-A-C.

Some cases will have more than one issue; when this happens, you should make sure to do a complete analysis for each issue.

❶ Statement of the issue

Formulating the issue is just as difficult as formulating the rule of the case; you have to make sure that your statement of the issue is neither too vague nor too specific. In many cases, the issue is really just the rule of law stated as a question. For instance, in *Garratt*, the issue could be restated as "has a person who knows with substantial certainty that some occurrence will result from her action committed an 'intentional' act?" Determining and stating the rule of the case will help you understand the issues involved in the case, and vice versa.

❷ Rule of law

This is the rule of the case you constructed earlier (see above).

❸ Rationale (application of the rule to the facts)

Carefully read the court's reasoning and pull out the critical points. Your reproduction of the court's arguments and reasoning should cover every major point raised in support of the holding. Most decisions can be broken down into two parts: (i) the court's analysis of precedent and its application to this case (does the case come within the precedents, can it be distinguished, should it be distinguished, or do the facts in this case dictate a reappraisal of existing law?); and (ii) application of the rule of the case to the facts of the case. You should focus on (ii), but don't ignore (i). While the background behind the rule of law may be of minimal importance on your exams, your professor may choose to explore it in her class discussion, and furthermore, your own sense of the structure of a subject will be enhanced if you know the development of existing law.

❹ Your Conclusion

The fourth element in the I-R-A-C format is the statement of your conclusion. This element is *critical* in exam answers, as discussed later in this book. In case briefs, however, your conclusion is about as important as the moon in daylight. The law is what the case says it is, not what you think it should be.

Book Briefing: An Alternative

Many students will find that a full briefing of cases is the most effective tool for building study discipline, and they will continue to brief cases throughout law school. However, to others, writing out a full brief for every case will become burdensome and they will look for easier alternatives. If that happens to you,

you have two options; you can either (a) book brief or (b) stop briefing altogether. Dismiss option (b) right now; omitting the organized analysis of your cases is a *bad idea*. Professors often rely on the analysis in a student's brief to drive the class discussion and raise points about a case. If you haven't done your own analysis, you'll be hard put to initiate or join in the discussion and you'll get less out of it. Failing to prepare a brief of any form is a disservice to yourself, your professor, and your classmates.

Option (a)—book briefing—is the art of writing the analysis of a case directly into your casebook. Book briefing is usually done either as you read the case for the first time or on a second pass through the case. As with a written brief, the end result of the book brief should be a well-organized analysis of the case.

There are several key elements to proper book briefing:

❶ effective *highlighting of text*;

❷ extensive *note-taking in the margins*; and

❸ a *coding system* to call out relevant facts, the issue, the rule of law, the rationale, the holding, and the like.

By the time you turn to book briefing, you should be trained to spot the relevant facts, issues, holdings, and so on. (If not, you may want to consider writing full briefs for a little longer, until you can spot those elements quickly and easily.) It's important to highlight the relevant facts of the case; that way, when the professor says, "Mr. Smith, please give me the facts of *White v. Benkowski*," you'll be ready to glance at your casebook and read from the highlighted portions. The same need to highlight applies to the issue(s), holding(s), and rationale(s) in the case.

Any important points not clearly identified in the text of the case should be written into the margins. This can include the holding and rationale for individual issues; it's often easier to write a two- or three-sentence condensation of the facts or ruling than to piece them together through ten or more pages of intermittent highlighting.

A good book brief needs a coding system to keep track of what's in the case. The most commonly used coding system is a system utilizing the letters **F** (facts), **PH** (procedural history), **R** (rule of the case), **I** (issue), **A** (application of law to facts), **C** (conclusion), and **D** (*dicta*). You should place the appropriate code in the margin of your book next to your written notes and highlights to mark the elements of your book brief.

Review

Reviewing is a vital part of the study process; however, reviewing will be effective only if you do it properly. Not only is inefficient reviewing a waste of time, but it's frustrating as well. If you review inefficiently, you'll feel that you've spent a lot of time without understanding or remembering what you've reviewed.

To study effectively, you should review at each of four stages:

❶ after you've read a case;

❷ at the end of each study session;

❸ just before class; and

❹ periodically, at the end of each topic you cover in class.

Reviewing at these four stages actually takes very little time but performs a crucial function: It prevents you from forgetting material at the times when forgetting most often takes place.

As you read the following discussion, notice that reviewing is an active process, a process that requires you to do exactly what you must do on your exams: recall information.

After Each Case

After you've read and briefed a case, take a blank sheet of paper and place it over your brief. Move the blank sheet down to reveal only the name of the case. Recite, preferably aloud, everything you remember about the case. (Reciting aloud forces you to pay careful attention to your thoughts and words, while reciting silently gives your mind the opportunity to wander.) Try to replicate your brief, reciting the facts, issue, holding, rules, and rationale (and dissent, if included). This should take only a minute or two. Then, look back at your brief to see what you missed. You may find that this review reveals gaps in your brief; if necessary, look back at the book to pick up any points you missed.

After You've Completed a Reading Assignment

Once you've finished reading, briefing, and reviewing every case in your assignment, review the cases again. You should be able to remember the main points of each case. This review is crucial because it's the single most effective way to prevent forgetting. It not only helps you see what you've learned but also "locks in" the material before you can forget it. Perhaps its most important benefit is that it saves time later. By retaining more now, you'll need to spend far less time rereading and reviewing later, and, just before exams, time will be extremely precious.

During this review, you should synthesize the cases; repeat the questions you asked yourself at the outset, and try to see how the cases interrelate. Performing this synthesis after each reading assignment will help your memory and increase your understanding. You'll be making sense of the material by relating it to other things you've learned.

Pre-Class Review

Pre-class review is the icing on the cake. Because the mind takes between two and ten minutes to warm up to a subject, it pays to arrive early for class. Spend the few minutes before class conducting a mental "warm-up," which will also enhance your retention of the material, by performing these two small tasks:

❶ review your notes from the previous class, and

❷ review your briefs for the upcoming class.

Remember also that professors usually make their most important points in the first few minutes and the last few minutes of class, so it's absolutely critical to arrive on time.

Periodic Review

Periodic review helps to cement material in your memory and provides an opportunity to relearn any material you may have forgotten. Reviewing periodically also helps you keep the material in perspective; it helps create an overview of the subject, increasing your understanding of how the material fits into the overall scheme of the course.

You may organize your periodic review in one of two ways. The first method is to establish a chronologically based review schedule; for example, you may decide to review every week, every two weeks, or once a month. The second method may be more helpful. With this method, you time your periodic reviewing to coincide with the end of each topic taught in the course; your review times are determined by substance, rather than by time. One benefit of substance-based review periods is that they take place at different times for different courses. You're unlikely to complete topics at the same time in every course, so your reviews will be staggered.

If you have a commercial outline or study aid, review it thoroughly as part of your periodic review for each topic.

Starting an Outline

Periodic reviews have another benefit: They help you to move from taking notes to producing an outline. (Outlining is covered in detail in Chapter 6.) For each major topic you review, you'll review the relevant subtopics, the rules under each subtopic, the rationales for those rules, and (very brief) examples. You should start drafting your outline as you start to review. Typically, students who perform badly on their first-semester exams report that starting their outlines too late in the semester was at least partly to blame.

To create an outline, you will use your class notes, supplementing them with any major points in your briefs that weren't discussed in class. You will likely write your outline using a word processing program, such as Microsoft Word. You may choose to use one of the program's preformatted outlines (a few minutes learning your computer's outlining software can save a lot of time later) or you may prefer to create your own format, but whichever way you choose, create it in such a way that makes it simple to insert, delete, and rearrange material within the outline. Be sure to set it up in a traditional outline format (or you'll just end up writing your notes over again).

If, for example, you start to outline defamation in torts, your outline might look like this:

A. DEFAMATION: Definition of defamation
    1. Subtopic A (e.g., Colloquium): RULE
        a. Rationale 1

      b. Rationale 2
2. Subtopic B: RULE
      a. Rationale 1
      b. Rationale 2
3. Examples from Briefs:
      a. *Case Name 1*: Example of defamation
      b. *Case Name 2*: Example of defamation
4. Hypotheticals:
      a. Professor's hypothetical from class X
      b. Professor's hypothetical from class Y

Another method of outlining may be to simply put the above material into one paragraph under "Defamation," and then start a new paragraph for the next topic. Remember: Format your outline in a way that makes it easy to move things around.

You may even want to take notes in an outline format during class if you are typing instead of handwriting your notes. Some students may find this too distracting, however, so make sure you are truly listening to the professor rather than worrying about putting information in the correct "slot." Furthermore, as discussed later in Chapter 5, Note-Taking and the Classroom Experience, it's important to pay close attention to what your professor says at the end of the semester. You must be able to easily add any information your professor mentions later on (include the date of the mention) and then incorporate it into a finished outline.

Reviewing Progressively

Even if you choose to conduct your periodic review chronologically (say, every two weeks), at the end of each major topic you cover in class you should review in "progressive parts." With progressive review, you learn one topic, then learn the next topic, and then study the two topics together. Subsequently, when you learn the next topic, you study all three together. Note that "studying" in this context doesn't mean poring over every note and case; you simply go over your outline. Studying in this way combats a major problem for many law students: their inability to see the relationships between the many topics covered in class. Studying progressively has the added benefit of demonstrating to yourself that you are, in fact, learning a lot. Also, if you review by "progressive parts," you are less likely to feel overwhelmed by material that you've covered but may not completely remember.

Reviewing with Electronic Media

If you have access to a digital recorder, recording software, and a CD burner, creating your own CD study aid is an effective way to learn since it forces you to focus on your materials and summarize them.

It also creates "dual coding" for your memory: You not only see material, but you hear it as well. CDs are especially useful in reinforcing key terms and statements. CDs are probably best made during your periodic reviews. Record important rules from cases, hypotheticals from your notes, and any other material you want to summarize; then, play the CDs while driving, getting dressed, exercising, or cleaning up. This can be particularly helpful if you are an auditory learner or have a particularly long commute.

Also, you should take advantage of podcasts and other free audio downloads on the Internet. Many schools offer podcasts on a variety of subjects, and you can also find relevant podcasts available on iTunes or other online audio retailers. However, keep in mind that any of these (unless created by your professor) should only be used to supplement your class work—it shouldn't replace it.

Reviewing with Flashcards

Most law students don't realize that flashcards are one of the *best* methods available for learning law. You can make your own, or use commercially available flashcards. There are also software programs that will turn your outlines into flashcards for you. (Simply use your Internet search engine to find what programs are available.)

The "traditional view" of studying has been that the only way to learn a subject is to read the major cases, statutes, and rules, and distill out the issues, holdings, and significance from each. This allows a student to construct the "big picture" of a subject. However, this is *not necessarily the most effective way to learn law.* Most other disciplines, such as business school and college courses, teach you the rules first, then use examples to reinforce the rules. The traditional method of learning law does the opposite: It gives you case after case, and expects you to be able to distill the rules from these cases. The traditional method does serve an excellent purpose—it teaches you how to *read and analyze cases.* However, the business-school-type approach to learning can be a much more efficient method of learning the law, and commercial outlines, hornbooks, flashcards, and other study aids follow this style.

Many students resist using flashcards because they feel that they are nontraditional and can't possibly help them to learn the law better than more conventional study aids. However, flashcards have four advantages over other types of study aids:

❶ they're *portable,*

❷ they break the law into *discrete chunks,*

❸ they can be *fun to use,* and

❹ they give you *practice applying rules of law to fact patterns.*

First, the flashcards you need for any one class or study session are much more portable than an outline or a hornbook. They fit well into a shirt or jacket pocket and can be used to create study time from wasted time (e.g., time spent sitting on a crowded train, walking on a treadmill, etc.). If you're trying to maximize your available study time, flashcards can be an excellent tool.

Second, flashcards break an area of law into discrete chunks of information, which makes the learning process easier (especially for first-year students). For instance, adverse possession is a complicated topic; there is generally a four-part test for adverse possession, and each element of the test has several sub-rules. Flashcards can be used to break this topic into smaller, more digestible chunks. For instance, you could have a single card that tests your memory of the four-part test (e.g., "What is the four-part test for adverse possession?"), followed by a number of individual cards covering the important points to remember about each part of the test, followed by hypothetical cards to test your overall knowledge of the subject of adverse possession.

Third, flashcards can be used to incorporate humor into the learning process. People tend to remember a memorable fact pattern better than the facts and holding of a particular case or a point of law. By incorporating humor into the learning process, your mind forms an association between the fact pattern and the point of law or case you're studying, and you'll remember more of what you study. Also, if you like games or are a naturally competitive person, you can use flashcards to turn studying into a memory "game."

Fourth, hypothetical flashcards serve a dual purpose; they help you to not only learn the law, but also give you valuable experience *applying law to a given set of facts*. After all, for your final exam, you'll have to apply the law you've learned to a given fact pattern. Answering a number of hypothetical questions on each topic is valuable practice for the all-important examination.

Some students will prefer to create their own flashcards. However, there are two main drawbacks to making your own flashcards: (1) they can be *time-consuming* to create and (2) writing good hypothetical flashcards is extremely difficult to do (it requires a commanding knowledge of the subject, which is what you're trying to gain by studying in the first place!). Consequently, you should consider using a set of *commercial flashcards*, and supplement it with your own additional cards covering class material either not covered by the flashcards or treated in more detail than in the flashcards. If you choose to make your own flashcards, there are three rules you should remember:

> **Ask questions, don't just regurgitate rules.** Flashcards should be an *active*, not passive, study tool. You're better off posing questions to yourself than just stating rules of law. For instance, if you were going to begin with a flashcard on the four-part test for adverse possession, the question side of the card should say, "What is the four-part test for adverse possession?" This question will force you to think, "What is it? Can I state and explain each part of the test?" You should NOT say, "List the four part test

for adverse possession," or something equally passive. The active approach forces you to *analyze, understand, and remember*, not just memorize.

Use mnemonics. For complicated rules with a lot of elements, try to think of a memory device to remember the elements. For example, a person can only claim title to land through adverse possession if the possession was *continuous, open and notorious, hostile and adverse*, and *exclusive*. A good mnemonic for this would be ECHO (**e**xclusive; **c**ontinuous; **h**ostile and adverse; **o**pen and notorious).

Try to make up good hypotheticals. Most law students who take the time to create a set of review flashcards create only flashcards on the black-letter rules of law. The real advantage of flashcards lies in applying those rules of law to a fact pattern. Thus, you should try to create a number of hypothetical flashcards that require you to apply the law to a given set of facts. If you can think up a number of fact patterns and understand how the law should apply to those facts, you'll be in great shape for the exam.

You may want to consider working in conjunction with a friend: Each of you can create a number of hypothetical cards, and then exchange them for review and criticism. This way, you not only both create flashcards, thereby drilling the concepts into your head, but you also get practice applying them to fact patterns you've never seen before.

Scheduling Study Time

If you're like most law students, you have more homework in law school than you ever had before. You may feel overwhelmed by the amount of work, but remember, you have the same amount of work as all the other students have, and you *will* be able to do it. If you schedule your time effectively, you will get your work done efficiently and still have time for a life outside of law school.

Using time well has its own benefits. If you create and follow a workable schedule, you will be able to finish your work in less time. Following a fixed schedule has a positive impact on grades; studies show that people who carefully plan their study time spend fewer hours studying and perform better on exams than people who don't budget their study time. In fact, people who don't schedule end up feeling that they have to study all the time. Remember Parkinson's Law: "Work expands to fit the time available for its completion." If you have all day to study but don't set up a specific study schedule, your work will take all day.

If you use the following guidelines, you'll spend far less time studying than your classmates and still perform better than they do.

Guidelines for Creating a Study Schedule

Tailor Your Schedule to Your Needs, Activities, and Personality

The most important element of an effective study schedule is that it be practical and workable. A good schedule doesn't ignore outside responsibilities and activities. "Outside responsibilities" obviously include a job or a family. However, these are not the only "responsibilities" you need to include in your schedule. If you like to play basketball on Wednesday, or don't want to miss Happy Hour at the local hangout on Thursday nights, or like to exercise three mornings a week, or want to have at least one day each week completely away from law (perhaps Saturday), don't create a study schedule that conflicts with these activities, or you'll feel too deprived to stick with it. Naturally, no matter how you arrange your schedule, you have to work the necessary number of hours, but depriving yourself of activities you truly enjoy is neither desirable nor necessary.

Don't Schedule an Unreasonable Amount of Study Time

When creating your schedule, don't pretend you're going to study every waking moment. A study schedule is like a diet: If you select one that allows you a carrot stick for breakfast, a celery stick for lunch, and a fish stick for dinner, sooner or later you'll abandon it. The same principle applies to studying. An unrealistic schedule cries out to be broken. If you tell yourself you're going to study every morning from 5 to 9, every night from 4 to midnight, and 12 hours a day on the weekends, you'll find every excuse to avoid studying. Remember, the purpose of a study schedule is to give you maximum freedom, not more work. Make sure your schedule does this. A good rule of thumb is to study three hours for every credit hour, basically treating law school like a 60-hour-per-week job—15 or so hours in class, 45 or so hours studying.

The Parameters of a Successful Study Schedule

No single study schedule is right for everyone; however, any study schedule should take into account several considerations.

Write Out a Weekly Schedule

Whether on a smartphone, on paper, on a Blackberry, or on your computer, the most successful schedules are actually written down. Don't just let things float around in your head.

Treat Law School Like a Job

The most successful law students treat law school like a 60-hour-per-week job. They get to law school at the same hour every morning and leave at the same time every night. Figure out what is a reasonable time for you to get to school, and get to school at that time every day whether you have class or not. Keep in mind your sleep patterns. If you need nine hours of sleep to function, you need to plan around it. With a 60-hour-per-week schedule, you should end up with about 60 hours available for sleep, 60 hours available for school, and about 60 hours available for friends, family, goofing-off, and other things. Play to your strengths—if you're a night owl, you can study more at night. If not, go to bed and plan on getting up in the morning. You should also try to incorporate regular exercise into your schedule (running, boxing, racquetball, etc.). Many studies have shown a strong link between memory, mood, and aerobic exercise. The hour or so you spend on the treadmill every other day will be time well spent.

Spread Out the Study Sessions

A striking research finding is that if you study something for one half-hour session per day for five days, your grades will be a full 25 percent higher than if you study the same material in a single two-and-a-half hour session, even though the total time spent studying is the same. Research also indicates that you learn more in three 30-minute sessions than in a single 2-hour session. Counterintuitively, you can study less and actually learn more.

Don't Do Your Reading Assignments Too Far in Advance

The more you remember from your reading assignment, the more you'll get out of class. If you do your reading assignments too far in advance of when the class meets, you'll remember so little of the material that you'll lose the benefits of working ahead. As a general rule, then, try to do assignments the day before they'll be discussed in class. This, together with a five-minute pre-class review (of your notes from the last class and your briefs of the current day's assignment), will maximize your classroom learning. (Of course, if you know in advance that you'll be busy the night before class, you'll have to work ahead; it's better to work in advance than not to prepare at all—you'll get even less out of a class if you haven't prepared for it at all.)

For a three-credit course, you should read and brief for about four to five hours per week. (The other four or five hours should be spent outlining, doing practice questions, and memorizing your outline.) A schedule can help you read more effectively by forcing you to do it within the time set aside for this task. For example, if you have two hours to read for Criminal Law, and you have four cases to read, you can spend about a half hour reading and briefing each case. While you'll start out slowly in your first semester, as you get more proficient at extracting what you need from each case, forcing yourself to stick to your schedule will encourage you to focus and read more effectively than if you have extra time to let your mind wander. This will help you pick up your reading and analytical speed, which will help you succeed even under the time pressure in exams.

Study Regularly

Simply put, studying the same subject at the same time in the same place every day makes studying easier. Why? Because studying only becomes easy when it becomes a habit. If, for example, you decide to study from 5 to 7 every evening, the routine and expectation of studying during that time will cause that studying to become a habit. Once formed, a habit becomes fixed and automatic, and you'll find that you're predisposed to study at that time every day. *Break up* your studying for each class and write down *exactly* what you should be doing at each time each week. For a three-credit course, you should read and brief for about four to five hours, outline for about two hours, do practice questions for about two hours, and memorize your outline for about an hour. Consequently, on your schedule, you need to write "Tuesday, 10-12, Outline Torts"—if you just write "Torts" or "Study," all you'll ever do is read, and success on your exams depends on you mastering the other necessary skills. If all you do is read, it's like expecting to know how to swim after only reading a book about it.

It's important to evaluate frequently your study schedule and adjust it if necessary. If you find you're not getting everything done, keep track of what you're doing every day. Are you spending more time than you thought procrastinating and surfing the Internet? Is your commute longer than you have scheduled? Do you spend a lot of time chatting in the library? Are you getting too little sleep? Are you getting too much sleep? Are you not scheduling any time for things you enjoy?

Tailor the Demands of Your Schedule to Your Personality

How precisely you schedule your study time depends on how much rigidity you can tolerate. Some people take comfort in—and can stick to—a very rigid schedule, one with every hour accounted for. A precisely detailed schedule is ideal, but only if you're the type of person who can live with it. At least try the precisely detailed schedule for a week, even if you've never tried one before.

If, however, a rigid schedule makes you uncomfortable, and you know you won't stick to one, then you'll need to create a more personal, flexible schedule. Here are two options.

✔ List What You Have to Do Each Day, and Check-Off Items as You Complete Them

Instead of a rigid time schedule, you may prefer the "daily list" method. Set aside "chunks" of time every day during which you plan to study. For example, you may decide to study for two hours every morning and two hours every evening. (It's not a good idea to study for longer than two hours at one sitting.) Depending on your class schedule, these "chunks" may occur at somewhat different times each day, and your schedule will be somewhat flexible.

Each evening, make a list of every bit of work you need to do on the following day: the pages you have to read, the notes you have to review, and every other task you must complete, no matter how small. As you complete each item on your list, cross it off. Getting through your list every day is critical to this method's success; don't use a flexible schedule unless you're able to avoid procrastinating.

✔ Create a Weekly Schedule

This is a variation on the "daily list" method described above. Create a weekly schedule that includes every major time commitment you have: classes, extracurricular activities, job, and any regularly scheduled social activity. Use this weekly schedule to create a daily "to do" list; then, cross off each task as you complete it.

Working Around Insomnia

Many law students have difficulty sleeping. If you have this problem, take it into account when planning your study time. Ideally, you should stop studying two hours before you go to bed and do something relaxing and completely unrelated to law: watch TV, play video games, read a mystery, relax with friends or family. Just don't think about law.

Also, don't study in bed. While it's tempting to study in bed, particularly if you live in a dorm, it will cause your mind to associate your bed, which induces sleep, with studying; studying means thinking, and thinking and sleep don't go well together.

If You Have to Study When You're Tired

Ideally, you should adjust your study time to mesh with your biological clock; if this isn't possible, however, and you must study when you're tired, try this: Elevate your feet and let the blood flow to your head; breathe deeply, slowly, and rhythmically; then, eat something sweet. These things will stimulate you and should help you study more effectively.

Scheduling Your Time Around a Family or a Full-Time Job

Entire books are devoted to advice on how to "juggle" your time efficiently in order to satisfy competing responsibilities. The following are a couple of basic ideas you can try.

If you have significant responsibilities outside of school, or if perhaps you're going to school at night, you probably have precious little free time. You'll have to create time as best you can. Make the most of commuting time and lunch hours by listening to lecture tapes or study tapes, or by studying flashcards (but not while you're driving to school).

Even though you have other commitments, you should still block out regular study sessions each week and try to commit two hours of study time per session. If possible, try to schedule your study periods so they take place just before and just after class. Before class, review your briefs and the notes from the last class; after class, review the notes you took. In this way, the material will be fresh in your mind during class, and you'll remember more afterwards.

Finally, keep in mind that you can't please everyone. If you've made a commitment to get through law school, you must use a certain amount of time to study and attend class. It may be difficult to convey your need for time to family members and friends, who may not understand why you have to be so wrapped up in what you're doing. If you schedule carefully, you can promise them blocks of time as well. However, if they truly want you to succeed, they will have to understand that studying law takes time, and that using study time productively is crucial to your success.

Anatomy of a Study Session
Avoid Pre-Study Rituals

This is a corollary to the rule on studying at regular times. If you don't spend that time actually studying, it's futile to block out fixed study times. For example, it does no good to tell yourself that you're going to study from 5 to 7 p.m. if, at 5 o'clock, you don't begin to study. If, instead, you prepare a snack, talk to your old friend Jack on the phone, then spend another 20 minutes staring at the ceiling, you're destroying the opportunity to develop the habit needed for study. In other words, don't allow other activities to interfere with your commitment to study unless you have thought about them and decided they have priority over the prime goal of study.

Avoid Studying Similar Subjects

Studying similar subjects one after the other creates mental interference between the subjects; that is, your mind may confuse elements of one subject with elements of another. To the extent possible, therefore, try to study similar subjects at different times; for example, don't study Criminal Law and Torts together, if you can avoid it.

In Each Study Session, Study the Toughest Subject First

If possible, start each study session with the subject you find most difficult. In this way, you'll attack that material when you're at your best. Also, once you've finished, you'll be more apt to stick to your study schedule, since the remaining subjects will be easier for you.

Review Previous Notes Before Starting Fresh Material

You should review your most recent class notes when you begin your first study session of the day. That way, yesterday's notes will become "set" in your memory before you begin something new, and the old material will be less likely to "interfere" with the new.

Avoid Distracting Noise When You Study

It's not necessary to study in total silence, especially if a complete lack of sound bothers you. You should, however, avoid distracting noise. The ideal background noise for studying is "white noise": low-level background sounds that actually mask outside distractions. The hum of a fan is "white noise," as is the sound of an aquarium pump. You can even buy machines and tapes that create white noise—the sound of waves crashing, a rain storm, a waterfall, or a babbling brook. Instrumental music is equally good. Some noises should be avoided—conversations, television, music with words—any sounds that encourage you to pay attention to them, instead of focusing totally on the material you're studying.

Take Frequent Breaks

It's not wise to study for hours on end without a break. You need short breaks to allow your memory to "consolidate" what you've studied. Ideally, study in stints of about 45 minutes each (or a little less), taking 5- or 10-minute breaks between the stints. The length of your study "stints" should reflect how long it takes you to settle down. If it takes you 15 minutes to settle down and get all your supplies in order, it may be counter-productive to take a break every 30 minutes.

In addition to your scheduled 5- to 10-minute breaks, you should take breaks whenever you feel fatigued. Be careful, though, to distinguish between fatigue and procrastination. Ask yourself this question: Have you been studying intensively, and are you now finding it hard to focus and concentrate? If so, you're fatigued and need a break. If not, you probably haven't really gotten down to work and are just looking for an excuse to goof off. In that case, resist the temptation to take a break. Giving in to these temptations will make it more difficult to build the "habit" of studying.

Motivating Yourself to Study: Handling the Urge to Procrastinate

Inevitably, some material in law school will be a deadly bore. Taking an active role in studying will go a long way toward minimizing the boredom, as will a strong desire to get good grades. There are, however, several techniques you can use to make material more interesting to you. People pay close attention to material that interests them, so these techniques should make your material easier to learn.

Create an External Focus for the Material

Teach the material to someone else. If you have a spouse or friends who are truly interested in seeing you succeed, try teaching it to them. You'll find yourself making the material more interesting in order to hold their attention. Another "external application" for the material is to transform it into some type of study aid. Making audio recordings for your "periodic review" is one way to do this.

Instead of Studying the Uninteresting Material, *Organize* It

People who can organize material instead of "studying" it learn it as well as, or better than, people who "study" it. See if organizing the material first makes it more palatable to you.

Try to Imagine What Someone Else Might Find Interesting About the Material

You've probably heard the saying, "One man's meat is another man's poison." This holds true for law school subjects. Perhaps the most unpopular subject during first year is Civil Procedure, yet some people (hopefully, your professor is among this group) find it fascinating. Students who like Civil Procedure often say that they consider it a puzzle and that they enjoy the challenge of figuring the elements out. If you intensely dislike any subject, try to put yourself in the shoes of someone who has learned to like it.

Create Rewards and Incentives for Yourself

Plan a pleasant activity—like watching your favorite TV program or going to your favorite restaurant—that you will allow yourself only after you achieve a specific, prescribed learning goal. This creates an "external" motivator for sticking with your goal.

Fight Hard to Avoid Wasting Time

Monsters lurk in your living room and kitchen, ready to devour you and your study time: the worst are the refrigerator, the Internet, the TV, and the telephone. If you analyze it, it will amaze you to discover how desperately you want to see every re-run of your favorite show, or how long it's been since you talked with your old friend, Rex, or how much you prefer a cold drink or your rollerblades to your studies. Beware! Monsters like these can doom law students.

If it's time to study, don't turn on the TV. If you simply can't miss a program, record it for later viewing. Reschedule plans you've made with friends; a true friend will sympathize with your plight. If you know you're prone to procrastinate, create the reward system described above: Treat yourself to something only when you finish studying, not before then. (You may think you're too sophisticated for a carrot-and-stick ploy, but, if you're tempted to procrastinate, you need to try anything and everything to overcome the urge to avoid work.)

Study for Just Five Minutes as Soon as You Get Home

Most people who procrastinate aren't lazy; they just can't bring themselves to start. If this is a problem for you, force yourself to spend five minutes studying when you get home from school—just five minutes. If you can't continue after five minutes, close your books, do whatever you want, and come back to your work later. If you force yourself to start, you may be able to continue until you finish; then, you can enjoy the rest of the evening guilt-free. Sure, it's a game and a deception, but it may become an easy habit for you, so it's worth a try.

Follow a Fixed Schedule for Just One Week; See if You Learn to Like It

Surely you can stand anything that will last only a week. Fix a firm schedule that you think you can keep for a whole week. Tell yourself you just have to stick with this schedule, and stay with it. When the week is over, you may find that it wasn't so bad. In fact, because you were so dedicated and productive, you may find that following your schedule actually gave you more free time than you would have had without it. You'll face another week of the same schedule without fear. If you continue taking one week at a time, you'll find that what felt like an overwhelming task—sticking to a fixed study schedule for the whole semester—has turned into easily digestible "bites."

Preparation for Legal Writing Courses or Moot Court

As mentioned earlier, most law schools require first-year students to participate in a moot court experience and take a Legal Writing seminar. Both of these courses require a significant amount of time, but the work should *not* be prioritized over studying for your other classes. The main reasons are because these are usually worth fewer credits and/or are graded on a pass/fail basis (e.g., a typical Legal Writing course is worth two credits, so spend six hours a week on it (two credit hours times three study hours per credit)).

A Legal Writing course is designed to teach you the basics of legal research and hone your legal writing skills. While you may fancy yourself the best writer of your generation, this class is not the forum for your creative prose. Your instructor will not be impressed when you write an extra five pages in iambic pentameter. Your instructor *will* be impressed with a well-researched brief submitted on time and within the specified page limits. A common practice is to push the writing assignment to the side until the day before it is due and then spend 14 hours pounding away at the keyboard. *Don't do this* for obvious reasons. A second mistake is focusing on the writing assignment instead of reading and preparing for Contracts or Civil Procedure or another core class because you enjoy writing and hate damages analysis. This is just as dangerous as procrastinating, and will cost you vital preparation, recital, and review opportunities.

A Legal Writing course may be worth fewer credit hours than your other classes. If so, spend proportionately less time on the work for that class without sacrificing the quality of your work. Importantly, you should add the work to your weekly schedule by breaking the writing assignment into manageable pieces. For example, spend so many hours on research, then so many hours on reading and outlining, and then the balance of hours on writing the final assignment. Spread it out over the week just as you would the studying for any other course. Some students begin to feel overwhelmed as they face writing assignments in addition to studying, class preparation, and outlining. You won't have to feel that way if you have adequately prioritized your time.

Legal Writing is a huge stumbling block for many students. First, it is likely the only class that will give you any feedback before exams, and, for that reason, you may start to hate it. Secondly, students sometimes get the idea that it is not as important as their other courses (although writing is the only thing you will be certain to do in your legal career—you may never see another Criminal Law case again). Third, legal writing is very formulaic and rigid, and you may need to "unlearn" much of what you learned in undergraduate (e.g., you might find yourself having trouble condensing your work, where in undergraduate you might have had trouble expanding it to reach a page limit). Fourth, many students who were good writers as undergraduates immediately assume that legal writing will pose no problems whatsoever. Don't fall into any of these traps. The best advice is to treat Legal Writing like your other courses—as a new experience you have limited familiarity with. Also, do not put off papers until the last minute (while extensions may have been granted to you as an undergraduate, you're not going to get them in law school). Third, take advantage of your Legal Writing professor's or writing specialist's office hours. Finally, plan out your schedule so you are never turning in the first draft of a Legal Writing assignment—make sure you do multiple drafts, get comments on them, and edit the assignment several times.

A moot court experience is generally pass/fail; therefore, this is definitely not the course on which to spend the majority of your time. It *is* the time to enjoy learning what appellate litigation is like and maybe to pretend that you are the top trial attorney on your favorite legal television show. Most students enjoy moot court (really!), but just as with your Legal Writing course, break the work into manageable pieces with set deadlines and *do not* prioritize it over your daily reading and class preparation. Remember that the top litigator in moot court still gets a "pass" and you must remain focused on the classes that will affect your grade point average the most. Spend just the amount of time that will allow you to complete your work well and on time without abdicating other responsibilities.

Study Traps to Avoid

There are a number of traps you can fall into while studying that will waste valuable time.

Don't Copy Over Your Notes!

You probably know students who carefully recopy the notes they've taken in class, word for word. You may even have done this yourself. Some people think there's something magical about recopying notes verbatim, as if this process will imprint the words in their memories. This is just not true. Effective studying requires that you take an active role in the process. It's easy to copy something word for word even though your mind has wandered to other things. Want proof? Answer this: Can you recopy your notes, word for word, while watching TV? Sure you can—and that means copying isn't an effective study technique. Copying notes is dangerous because it can trick you into believing you're studying; you rely on it because it takes a lot of time, and it's directly related to what you're studying. But be forewarned. It doesn't contribute to better grades, and anything that doesn't improve your grades isn't worth the time or the effort; ultimately, it will just leave you feeling frustrated.

Don't Reread Your Text and Notes Again and Again

Research has consistently shown that reading your text and notes once and then concentrating to *recall* the material is far more effective than reading it over and over. Remember, each step in your studying is like a rocket booster: As soon as a step has served its purpose, it should fall away. Once your briefs and class notes are in good shape, don't spend a lot of time rereading. Rather than rereading, take an active role in reviewing by asking yourself questions suggested by your notes.

Don't Be Discouraged by Thick Books or Imposing Assignments

Yes, you're going to have to read 1,000 + pages of Property in your first year, and perhaps the same number of pages in each of your other classes. In fact, you'll read more than 5,000 pages of material in your first year of law school!

If your exams were going to be held tomorrow or next week, you would be justified to feel discouraged, but they're not. Remember, all that matters now is what you have to do *right now*. Your short-term goals are relatively small and attainable. You don't have to read 1,500 pages tonight—or even 150. If you divide 5,000 pages among 200 school nights, you have only 25 pages per night! Even when exam time arrives, you won't have 1,500 pages to review; you'll need to review only your outline and flash cards. As with any goal, you'll have intermediate targets that you'll be able to meet. As the saying goes, a journey of a thousand miles begins with a single step. If you can resist the temptation to procrastinate, you won't be overwhelmed by the demands on your time.

By the same token, you do have a relatively large amount of studying to do. If you had a tendency to "cram" in college, get out of the habit *quickly*. The volume of material can become overwhelming if you don't keep up each day.

If you miss an assignment or two, try to rely on outlines and commercially prepared briefs to fill the gap—don't go back to the source at first. If you force yourself to read the text you missed, you may end up locked in place—you may feel overwhelmed by the amount you have to do; the more overwhelmed you feel, the more paralyzed you'll be. You may fall perpetually behind, which isn't productive and will hurt you in class. If you've dropped the ball, pick it up with today's assignments. Only after you've finished them should you even try to fill in gaps. Missing any single assignment won't hurt your grade if you move forward aggressively. If you do fall behind, the best advice is to borrow notes from your friends and read just enough of the cases that you failed to read to be able to create an effective outline (namely, a brief idea of the facts and the black letter law presented by the case).

If a Crisis Occurs

If a personal crisis occurs, discuss it immediately with your dean of students or academic support professional; you may be able to rearrange your exam schedule to accommodate the crisis. You may even be able to postpone some classes until the summer. Don't be a martyr. If you need help, ask for it. Your career as a lawyer may well depend on a realistic approach to personal problems that interfere with good study habits.

Reviewing Your Notes

Reviewing your notes regularly is an essential part of using them productively. Too often, students who've taken good notes make the mistake of waiting until just before the exam to review them. By that time, the notes will have lost much of their meaning.

Your goal is to score as many points as you possibly can on your exams. Research indicates that reviewing your class notes will result in higher grades. The following are some tips for making your review as effective as possible.

When to Review

Conduct a Ten-Minute Review as Soon After Class as You Can; Never Delay Longer than 24 Hours

This may strike you as a waste of time, but it's not. The minutes you spend on this "quick review" will save you hours later on. This review solidifies information that might otherwise quickly evaporate. A ten-minute review will help transfer the information in your notes from your short-term memory into your long-term memory. Research indicates that, without this review, students recall less than 20 percent of a class's content a day later.

Periodic Review: After an Important Topic Has Been Covered in Class, Review Your Notes on It from the Beginning

First, identify each major topic covered; you can do this either by referring to the topic headings in your text or by creating your own index of case names and key words. Take each key word or topic in order, recite everything you can about it, then check your notes and see what you've missed.

How to Review

You are making a serious (and extremely common) mistake if you believe that "reviewing" your notes means reading them over and over. As discussed, copying your notes over and over doesn't help much, either. You will improve your grades only if your review is an active process requiring at least three elements: concentration, reflection, and recitation (either quietly or aloud).

Concentration

This is the other side of the no-procrastination coin. Once you sit down to work, address all your thoughts and energies to the one goal—learning the day's work (a set schedule will help with this—

if you know you only have two hours to accomplish something, you'll make yourself focus and accomplish it in those two hours). If you have ever concentrated hard on any one project or lesson, you know the satisfaction that comes from being "in control." Try to duplicate this process and experience every day—eventually, it will become second nature.

Reflection

For your daily review, concentrate and reflect on the major topic covered during that day's class. Ask yourself: Did I understand the "meat" of the session? Are there gaps in my notes that I need to fill in? What do I need to work on? For your periodic review, do the same, and add: Can I see the whole picture, and do I have a good understanding of how this topic fits in? If you answer "no," turn to a secondary source for help.

Recitation

Pretend that you're the professor and that you have to create exam questions based on the day's notes (or the major topic you're reviewing). What issues would you test? What questions would you ask? How would you phrase the questions to get at the heart of the issues? Once you've made up the questions, ask and answer them, aloud. (If you've joined a study group, the group is a perfect place for this "recitation.") Stating a question aloud, to yourself or to others, is important because this forces you to think. If you don't have to put your thoughts into sentences, it's all too easy to let your mind wander and to be imprecise and sloppy in your analysis of the work.

Study Groups: Advantages and Disadvantages

Many students believe that belonging to a study group is a fundamental solution to success in law school. While some people do gain a great deal from studying in a group, you may not. Here are some considerations to keep in mind if you're considering forming or joining a study group.

You May *Not* Want to Join a Study Group

There are several factors that weigh *against* joining a study group.

You May Be More Productive When You Study Alone

One of the goals in this book is to help you spend less time studying but still improve your grades. If you follow the strategies outlined here, you'll be very successful. Importantly, there does not seem to be any correlation between performance on exams and participation in a study group. If you suspect you'll have an easier and more comfortable time on your own, don't bother to try a study group. Trust your instincts. If you haven't used a study group before, you're probably well advised not to start in law school, where so much is at stake.

People Study in Different Ways

Everyone has unique study habits. Everyone studies at a different speed. Not everyone can study at the same time of day or night. In light of the pressure law school brings, many people will be better off studying alone. You know yourself better than anyone else. If you've always studied effectively alone, say "no" when you're asked to join a group.

You May Be Tempted to Slack Off if You Join a Group

Interaction with others can be an important element of effective studying. A well-functioning study group whose members quiz each other regularly on material covered in class can offer this benefit in abundance. However, it's possible to turn to a study group for the wrong reasons. For example, some students join so that they can swap outlines and avoid having to prepare their own. In the first year of law school, it's important not to fall into this trap.

In the second and third years of law school, you may be able to get away with swapping outlines or, alternatively, having each member of a study group prepare a different part of an outline. While you're still a first-year student, though, you must do the work yourself. Using the strategies in this book, the outlines you prepare will be far more valuable than anything you could get from your study group. Certainly, if swapping outlines is your primary purpose for joining a study group, don't join one. You won't be missing anything.

Characteristics of an Effective Study Group

Once you've debated the pros and cons of study groups, you may still want to organize or join one. Here are some tips to help you get the most out of a group.

Clarify Ground Rules at the Beginning

A study group should not add more stress to your life. To avoid this, make sure all members of the group agree to the ground rules before you even begin. Can people bring food? Can members be in more than one study group? Who is in charge during group sessions? Can members share group notes with other groups? What can get you kicked out of the group?

Choosing the Right Members

All members of a study group should be equally motivated and have similar levels of ability. When choosing members, try to avoid the pitfalls associated with committees: One or two people do all the work, and the other members simply take advantage of them. Also, learn to protect yourself. If you follow the study techniques explained in this book, your reputation as a scholar will spread and other students will look to you for good notes and outlines. While there's nothing wrong with helping people who understand less than you do, you must not let this interfere with your own studies. Less conscientious students rarely have anything to offer more conscientious ones.

Unfortunately, choosing the right study group is not much easier than avoiding genetic defects: The best way to live to a healthy old age is to be careful in choosing your parents. And the best way to create a good study group is to pick good study partners. But just as it's impossible to pick your parents, it's often impossible to identify students who are properly motivated or who can work at your speed. If you find yourself in a group with students you can't work with, think enough of yourself to withdraw, gracefully, as soon as possible. Don't be intimidated by the possible social consequences. This is not the time to do less than your best.

Choosing the Right Number of Members

Remember: The smaller the study group, the better. Even if you have only one study partner, you'll still receive most of the benefits of a larger group. You can still exchange questions and critique each other's work. Further, it's easier to schedule a smaller group than a larger one, and the members are more likely to have compatible study habits.

When You Should Form a Study Group

Most people expect to join a study group at the beginning of their first semester. This is actually the worst time to join one. Not only will you have no idea which students share your skills and study habits, but there's little benefit in intense group interaction until closer to exam time. A study group is most useful in preparing for tests. If you have winter exams, try to form a group at the end of October; if you have no exams until spring, wait at least until March to join a group. Remember, even one good group session, if properly timed, will be beneficial. Before the proper time, the disadvantages of spending your study time with others outweigh the advantages.

Stay Focused

You know the scenario: A few friends get together to study, sit down, and open to their notes. But just before they get started, someone says, "Can you believe Professor Farkus? I can't believe he said. . . ." Before you know it, you've spent an hour discussing everything but your assignment. While socializing is a necessary element in any law school schedule, it has nothing to do with studying. It's extremely frustrating to set aside three hours of your valuable time to study with your group, only to end up getting little done. Why not plan to get all your work done first and then socialize, preferably in a pleasant setting (perhaps at a local restaurant)? In that way, you'll associate your study time and location with work, not play.

Making the Most of a Study Group

When a study group is functioning perfectly, it will sharpen your ability to pull information from your memory. Whether you're formulating questions or answering them, you'll reap this benefit. To help accomplish this, you should consider the following.

Preparing Questions Beforehand

To insure that the question-and-answer session will be particularly useful to you, don't try to create questions on the spot during the study session. Instead, arrive armed with questions you've prepared in advance dealing with the material you've covered in class.

Taking Old Exams and Critiquing Each Other's Answers

Use the guidelines in Chapter 8, Test-Taking, to critique each other's practice answers. As discussed earlier, don't use old exams until shortly before your own exam. (Using them earlier will only serve to make you feel lost in material you haven't learned yet.)

Choosing Commercial Outlines and Other Study Aids

There are about 400 different law school study aids. Your law school bookstore will stock the most popular ones. If you don't find what you want, ask the store to order it for you. The bookstore buyer is only human. Her judgment on which study aids to stock may not always be the best. Student interest will influence the buyer's choices, so don't hesitate to let the buyer know what you want. And if you can't get what you want at the bookstore, contact the publisher directly.

Several publishers offer outlines of all the first-year subjects. You'll probably want to test a number of outlines before you settle on one publisher. Even if you don't buy all the outlines at first, it's reassuring to know that help is available.

With all the options available, sometimes it's hard to choose what's right for you. Choosing one is a matter of studying the field. The most popular outline series are the Emanuel Law Outline series and the series published by Gilberts. The Emanuel Law Outlines cover 17 subjects, including seven first-year subjects. The Gilberts outlines also cover most law school subjects. Other outlines and study aids are published by Lexis/Nexis, West, and Sum and Substance.

Before deciding which study aids to buy, spend some time in your law school bookstore becoming familiar with the various options. You may want to consult the bookstore manager to find out what's popular at your school. It should go without saying, but if your professor wrote a study aid on the subject you're taking from him, buy that study aid! In the last analysis, you should buy what appeals to you. You may even be influenced by such factors as the size of the book, the size of type, the book's format, and the various features offered by the publisher—these are all reasonable concerns.

The one important thing is to recognize that outlines are useful tools for most students, no matter what an occasional die-hard professor may say to the contrary.

You will also want to investigate the other types of study aids available, including CDs, Internet downloads, or bundled software. Each has its advantages, and only you can decide which one will help you the most.

Ultimately, the best place to go for advice on commercial study aids is your school's academic support professional. She may have a lending library of study aids, and she has years of experience in what works best for her students.

Using the Internet as a Law School Resource

Most law students don't realize it, but there's a vast quantity of law-student-related information and material available for free on the Internet. Many Web sites offer class outlines, old exams, tips from former and present law students, and much more. Internet newsgroups and Web site forums/discussion groups are excellent ways of getting in touch with fellow law students around the country.

Resources on the Internet

The Web was created as a tool for sharing information. Law students and law schools have taken advantage of the Web and made many of their course outlines, notes, exams, and the like available to anyone, anywhere. Additionally, many podcasts are available for free on iTunes. If you're looking for an outline for the eighth edition of Field, Kaplan & Clermont's *Civil Procedure* casebook, for example, you'll probably find one on the Web somewhere. If you want to pick up a couple of old exams for Contracts, but have already worked through everything in your law school library, you'll probably find others somewhere on the Internet.

One caveat: The biggest drawback of using student resources found on the Web is that you can't be sure of the quality of the material. Almost everything available for free on the Web was written by law students who weren't thinking about making their outlines and notes available to the masses when they wrote them. There's no assurance that the outlines you find will be complete or accurate. There is some quality stuff out there, but you should carefully review any study aid you find on the Internet before relying on it.

Search Engines

If you are not already familiar with the Internet, you'll need to use a search engine to find information useful for law students. The World Wide Web is a vast place. There are literally *millions and millions* of Web pages out there, only a few of which have information useful to you. Instead of "riding the information super-highway" with no particular destination in mind, let the search engines do the initial narrowing for you. For instance, enter "constitutional law outline," and within seconds, the engine will search the entire Internet and find all Web pages containing references to constitutional law outlines. If you're looking for specific information, but you don't know the URL of a Web site that is likely to have that information, a search engine is exactly what you should use.

Here are some of the most popular search engines on the Web:

✎ **Google (http://www.google.com).** Google is the world's largest search engine and will return thousands, if not millions, of hits on your search terms. While many of the hits will not be relevant to your needs, "Googling" your terms can help you find new ways to narrow down your search even further. For example, entering "constitutional law outlines" into Google returns 151,000 hits, but it also directs you to a Web site specifically geared toward law students and legal professionals, FindLaw (http://www.findlaw.com). If you have a general idea of what you are looking for, enter the general terms into Google and use the hits to narrow your search.

✎ **AltaVista (http://www.altavista.com).** AltaVista will also turn up more "hits," or Web sites containing some variation of your search terms, than you can realistically sift through in a short period of time. If you have a specific search, however, AltaVista works extremely well.

✎ **Yahoo! (http://www.yahoo.com).** Yahoo! is a general combination yellow pages/search engine; you can either search Yahoo! for a particular term or terms, or browse through its directories.

These four search engines should provide you with enough searching power to locate even the most hard-to-find Web sites. Remember, the more specific you are with your search request, the fewer bad "hits" you'll have to sift through before you find what you're looking for. Also, there are at least another dozen good search engines available on the Web. (Yahoo! has links to most of them.)

Other Useful Web Sites

Many schools, companies, and individuals have created Web sites containing a wealth of information and resources for first-year law students. Below are a few of the better ones. (**Note:** some of these sites may have moved or disappeared since this book was published.)

✎ **FindLaw (http://www.findlaw.com).** FindLaw has a very similar layout to Yahoo!, with both a search engine and direct links to information of interest to law students. One of the things you'll find at FindLaw is a section on law schools, which includes a subject-by-subject listing of student outlines available for download. It also has a directory of law student resources available on the Web; it's a good jumping-off point if you want to start surfing for outlines or old exams.
In addition, it has a complete A-to-Z listing of law school Web sites. Because many law schools post copies of released exams, some with sample answers, it's a good place to browse for old exams.

✎ **The 'Lectric Law Library's Study of Law Study (http:// www.lectlaw.com/study.html).** The 'Lectric Law Library is an excellent Internet resource for law students and attorneys. The "Study of Law Study" section is full of useful, free information and resources for law students, especially first-year students. The "Legal Research Guides" section contains free guides to help you learn how to do legal research; you can download primers such as "How to Shepardize" and "Ten Easy Steps to Legal Research." It also has a complete section of free, downloadable student outlines, as well a complete section of free student-written case briefs and a small selection of old exams.

✎ **The Legal Information Institute (http://www.law.cornell. edu).** Sponsored by Cornell University Law School, this site offers a legal search engine, many codes and statutes, and an introduction to basic legal citation.

✎ **The Center for Computer-Assisted Legal Instruction (CALI) (http://www.cali.org).** The Center for Computer-Assisted Legal Instruction is a consortium of law schools that researches and develops computer-mediated legal instruction. The site includes lessons on almost every conceivable law school topic and a link to Lawdibles (http://lawdibles. classcaster.net), a blog containing short audio lectures on many law school subjects.

✎ **Westlaw (http://www.lawschool.westlaw.com).** This site provides students with many tips and tools, including pointers on how to do your best in Legal Writing.

The LAWSCH-L Discussion List

There's one other legal resource on the Internet worth discussing—the LAWSCH-L discussion list. It's an Internet newsgroup devoted entirely to, and mostly populated by, law students. It's an easy way to reach out to your peers when you want to bounce an idea off them or you want to draw on an upperclass student's knowledge and expertise. The newsgroup works like a bulletin board; you can "post" a message to the newsgroup and then others can read your message and post a follow-up message, or respond to your message directly via e-mail.

The best way to access the law school discussion list is through Usenet, a collection of thousands of "newsgroups" on pretty much every topic imaginable. To access Usenet, you'll need a news browser; a news browser is included with the major Web browsers, such as Internet Explorer. Also, the major online providers, such as America Online (AOL) and Google Groups, provide access to Usenet newsgroups. The URL of the newsgroup is *bit.listserv. lawsch-l.*

CHAPTER 5

Note-Taking and the Classroom Experience

Taking Notes

Written properly, notes can make reviewing and outlining simple; they can also perform an even more important role: spotlighting what will appear on your exams. What you hear in class is more important than what you read. Taking good notes in class can increase your exam grades in four principal ways.

❶ **Exam Preparation**

Your notes will tell you what the professor considers to be important, and thus what she is most likely to test on the exam. Keep your exams in mind as you take notes and focus on writing things that will help you achieve your highest possible scores (e.g., any processes the professor uses—"This is the way to break down negligence: First, is there a duty? Second, is there a breach? . . .").

❷ **Memorization**

Taking and reviewing notes helps cement the material in your memory, so you're more likely to recall it.

❸ **Clarity**

Good notes help clarify points in the cases that you may have overlooked or found confusing.

❹ **Involvement**

When you take notes, you're forced to take an active role in summarizing what's being said. Consequently, taking notes transforms passive listening into active learning. Active learning is the foundation of effective studying.

How to Take Good Notes
Where to Sit

Sit as close to the front and to the center of the classroom as possible. Most students avoid doing this; after all, it's natural to feel some reluctance about sitting in a conspicuous spot. Research has shown, though, that students who sit in the front and in the center actually perform better on exams than students who sit in the back. Here are some possible explanations for this somewhat surprising result.

Boring Professors Can Seem More Interesting When You Sit Closer to Them

Some professors seem boring because their personalities don't project well in a large classroom. If you sit in the first few rows, you will be able to hear better, your attention span will increase, and you'll get more out of the class.

Sitting Near the Front Reduces Interference and Helps You to Focus on the Professor

The only important focus points in a class are your professor and the occasional student who's called upon to recite. You don't want to be distracted by anything else. If you sit at the back of the room, there are scores of things within your range of vision that can distract you (namely everyone else's laptop screens). If you sit toward the front, the potential distractions are narrowed to a very few. You're forced to concentrate on the professor and what he is saying.

It's Harder to Fall Asleep if You Sit in the Middle of the Front Row

If you want to remain inconspicuous, falling asleep in the back row isn't the way to do it. But the temptation to sleep is greater if you think you can get away it. If you sit up front, your sense of embarrassment and your increased concentration will help keep you awake. Sleep destroys your ability to learn. (It can also lead to a sharp rebuke and a stiff neck.)

By the way, don't believe the myth that people who sit in front are called on more often than those who don't. Professors know that students believe this, so they often make a point of calling on students who hide in the back. Also, many professors simply pick a starting point in the class roll and go alphabetically from there, so where you sit won't make a difference.

Note-Taking Tools

If you take notes by hand, use a loose-leaf notebook for your notes, not a spiral binder. With a loose-leaf notebook, you can shift and reorganize notes later and insert notes from any classes you may have missed. Also, if you keep all your notes in a single binder with dividers, you'll have all your notes in one notebook and not run the risk of picking up the wrong binder. Make sure you carry several pens with ink that won't smudge. The most frustrating thing in the world is to want to write and not be able to.

More likely, you will choose to type your notes on a computer or on a personal digital assistant (PDA) with attached keyboard. Save your lecture notes to your hard drive as you type and *back up your hard drive* on disks or CDs on a regular basis (or e-mail your notes to yourself). If you use a PDA, download the notes every night to your hard drive and then save to disks or CDs. Every semester, one of your classmates' computers will crash, freeze, get stolen, or the like and that classmate will not have saved her hard drive's information. *Don't be that student!* You don't want to have to rely on someone else's notes because yours are lost forever. Carry extra drives or CDs with your laptop.

A Note About Your Computer

Computers can be a fantastic tool, but as you probably know, they can also be a fantastic distraction. When you are in class, turn off e-mail alerts, shut down any Web pages you have open, and avoid getting into "chats" with your fellow students. You've probably paid a lot (in either time or money) to be sitting in this classroom—don't waste it by shopping or playing solitaire.

Format

Be sure to date all your notes. The sequence of material will ultimately be important, as you'll see in the section below on "Review."

Although you may prefer a different method, one note-taking format that's often recommended and has proven effective is the "Cornell format." To take notes by hand in this format, first draw a 1½" margin on the left-hand side of each page (some notebook paper comes with a vertical rule already there); then, write all of your class notes to the right of the line. The left margin is reserved for key words, topic headings, sample questions, rules, case names, words defined in the body of your notes, and the like. Across the bottom, draw another 3″ margin; on this part of the page, write down the "topic" or main points of the class discussion (so you can search quickly through your notes). This format makes finding things and later review easier, as discussed in detail later in this chapter. Most computer programs also have a Cornell format template. For example, in Microsoft Office, if you click to create a new document, you have the option of choosing a template—go down to "More Categories" and then "Notes." There are also several Web sites that can create Cornell templates for you for free.

Take your notes in paragraph form, leaving an extra space whenever the professor moves on to a new point. You'll find it easier to summarize your notes later if you insert breaks between points or ideas. Alternatively, if outlining comes naturally to you, you may choose to take notes in outline form, using headings and subheadings. You may find, though, that the content and complexity of law school classes will make instant outlining difficult and frustrating. Remember, there's no advantage to forcing yourself to take notes in outline form if it doesn't come naturally to you.

And, remember, the commercial outlines that are available have already organized the material for you. It's not a bad idea to borrow their headings and subheadings in arranging your notes. Another organizational method is to follow the table of contents in your casebook. As you arrive at a new section in your reading, open a new section in your notes and organize accordingly. You could also organize your notes using your professor's course syllabus. This format lends itself easily to outlining later in the semester. Finally, another possibility is organizing your notes following a case method. This works best in classes such as Civil Procedure. You begin with the notes and cases addressing the filing of the petition and finish with the notes and cases addressing the final appeal. This format provides a quick and easy "issue checklist," which you can use on exams. (Checklists are discussed in Chapter 6, Outlining.)

Note-taking and review will be easier and faster if you organize your notes with graphics. For example, you can use parentheses, circles, squares, flags, or any other visual means of grouping related information together. You can use stars, moons, hearts, asterisks, arrows, underlining, or any other symbols you invent to highlight important points. You can also use recurring symbols—they speed note-taking and help speed up recognition and review. For example, you're probably already familiar with the use of the symbol for "defendant" or for "plaintiff." If you don't like these, you can design your own. Other symbols you may want to use include:

∴	to indicate "therefore"
w/	to indicate "with"
w/o	to indicate "without"
↑	to indicate a factor likely to create liability
↓	to indicate a factor likely to diminish liability

Of course, typing may limit some symbols, but you can certainly use the Insert, Symbol function (in Microsoft Word) to tailor your notes.

Some students also create their own, easily-deciphered shorthand, such as eliminating vowels from words (e.g., "decision" becomes "dcsn"; "rationale" becomes "rtnl"). That's fine. But be careful to use the shorthand and symbols consistently and to make note of any new ones in your notes. Otherwise, when you review, you may not remember what a symbol was supposed to mean.

Our final note about formatting applies only if you are taking notes by hand, and you're a "doodler." If you doodle, you can actually use your artistry to help improve your grades. While your professor is busy grilling another student, illustrate your notes with drawings based on the case under discussion (e.g., a kid yanking a chair out from under someone to represent *Garratt v. Dailey* and "intent" for Torts). This "dual coding" will help cement the facts of the case in your mind; that is, you'll have not only the verbal record of the facts in your brief, but a visual image as well, so you'll be more likely to recall the facts later. (Be careful, however, not to be scribbling such "case pictures" when you should be taking notes on items being discussed; the advantage of the picture-graphs won't outweigh the disadvantage of missing an important point the professor is making.) If you do choose to draw, draw in the margin only. Keeping your notes pristine will make reviewing and summarizing them later much easier. You won't have to wade through a sea of flaming jet planes or geometric shapes in order to decipher your notes.

What to Write Down

Deciding which facts to record is at the heart of the note-taking process. This section began by discussing the advantages of good notes. One advantage is that you're storing information that you can use later to review for your exams.

Law students have widely varying styles of note-taking. Some type furiously, recording every word the professor utters; others take a few cryptic notes and call it a day. The problem with both extremes is that each fails to encourage you to take an active role in learning. If you record every word, you aren't identifying or concentrating on what's important. To take the best notes, you should take an active role in sorting through and summarizing what is said. Don't fall prey to either of the two most common fears students have: some fear they'll miss an important point if they don't write everything down; conversely, others fear that note-taking will interfere with their ability to absorb what is said. Neither of these is true.

Most professors speak at a rate of about 100 words per minute. Most students think at a rate of about 400 words per minute. You have plenty of time to digest and record what's being said, as long as you know what to listen for.

Some words of caution about voice-recognition software: as this technology improves, it may be tempting to purchase the software that will "type" every word the professor says while you sit back and contemplate what flavor coffee you're going to get after class. The danger is that it will be too easy for you to stop actively listening and you won't be able to filter the infor-mation from the lecture and format it into notes that will help you later as you study. While you may think that the software will free you up to concentrate on the lecture, think hard about why you want the program and make sure it isn't really to free you up to decide between French vanilla and mocha almond.

Basic Items that Should Appear in Your Notes

Four elements become the basic features of excellent notes. In general, your class notes should contain only those elements. Limiting your notes this way forces you to pick up nuances that indicate what will appear on the final exam. You should think of these nuances as "pearls." But first, you need to identify the four basics elements of effective notes.

❶ Hypotheticals Posed by the Professor

Why is it so important to write down the professor's hypotheticals? "Hypos" represent the occasions when the professor asks you to analyze facts in a question format. Facts in question format are exactly what you'll face on your exams, and your professor's hypos are usually the prelude to his own exam questions.

How should you take notes on hypos? If you use the Cornell format, write the hypo itself in the left column and its answer in the body of your notes. If you don't use the Cornell format, be sure to highlight hypo questions in some clear and emphatic way, such as enclosing them in boxes or underlining them.

❷ The Rationales and Public Policies Behind the Rules

Rationales and public policy questions are important for two reasons. First, they help you to understand the rules of law, and this understanding is one of the keys to exam success. Second, they help you to remember the rules; if you can't remember a rule, "thinking around it" will often cue your memory. One way of "thinking around a rule" is to identify its rationale or public policy goal.

The rationales behind rules are crucial to the analysis of exam questions. Many exam questions involve "gray areas"—that is, areas not clearly settled by any single, specific rule. When dealing with a gray issue question, the ability to identify and discuss the policy and rationales behind all potentially applicable rules will help you to determine which rules ought to apply and then to justify your choices—factors crucial to scoring a high grade.

❸ Definitions and Rules

These are the exceptions to this book's advice about limiting yourself to summaries. You should take down every word of a definition or rule, especially if the professor repeats the wording several times. Putting her words down verbatim ensures that you have her view on each rule and definition. You'll score better if you're able to recite her definitions and rules precisely on your exam, and recording them verbatim in class is the first step toward doing that.

Pay particular attention when a professor restates a rule she has previously covered (for example, she may restate the definition of battery in a later session dealing with murder). The definition *as your professor restates it* is, if anything, even more important than the way she stated it originally. The way your professor restates the rule is the way you want to remember it, too.

❹ Case Names and Conclusions

When a case you read the night before is discussed in class, refrain from writing notes until the discussion is over. Write the case name down (in the left column, if you use the Cornell format), then stop writing while your classmates are quizzed about it. You hardly ever need to write down comments made by your classmates.

Remember, you're taking notes only for the purpose of reviewing them later. You won't need to review the discussion of cases or your classmates' comments because you won't be tested on them. Wait until a rule is developed or a conclusion is reached, and then write the rule or conclusion below the case name, along with any explanation you feel is necessary—for instance, the facts of the case and its underlying rationale or public policy.

What if There Is No Conclusion?

The nature of the Socratic method used in most classes means that, for certain cases, the professor will never actually supply his own conclusion at the end of the discussion. He will either forget to state one or decide that you should figure it out yourself, and he will move on to the next case. When this happens, you should do three things:

❶ Make a note of the fact that no conclusion was reached,

❷ use a secondary source (commercial study aid or hornbook) to determine and note the correct conclusion, and

❸ listen carefully for a review of the material later in the course. You may hear a conclusion then.

Inevitably, during presentation of subsequent topics, the professor will refer to an earlier discussion of cases or principles needed for an understanding of the new material. When this occurs, he will, necessarily, either restate the conclusion supplied in an earlier discussion or state a conclusion missing from the earlier discussion. Listen carefully for statements such as, "Remember our discussion of felony murder? The rule there was. . . ." Be sure to write down his statement of the conclusion and highlight it in your notes. Later, when you review your notes, add his conclusion into the earlier discussion of the case, if it's missing. Remember to incorporate it into your course outline as well (which you should start as soon as you've covered enough information in class to make an outline).

"Pearls" You Should Include in Your Notes

"Pearls" are those significant nuances that communicate what will appear on your exams. The more pearls you record, the better you'll do. You must learn to spot the physical and verbal cues that your professor gives you.

Verbal Cues

Verbal cues include:

Words that Constitute Signals

Whenever your professor starts a sentence with transitional words like the following, it's a good idea to listen carefully and write down whatever comes after them:

"The following four factors . . ."

"In conclusion . . ."

"The most important consideration is . . ."

"In addition to . . ."

"On the other hand . . ."

"The major cause is . . ."

"Two ways to determine X are . . ."

"The difference between . . . and . . . is . . ."

and the most obvious one:

"This will be on the exam. . . ."

These are all words of introduction, transition, and conclusion: They indicate that the professor is about to sum up, in her own words, what's been said, and they highlight material likely to appear on the exam.

The Professor Refers to His Recent Book or Article

Your professor is likely to test you on those topics he finds interesting. His articles or books definitely reveal his interests. If you're lucky enough to hear your professor mention his publication in class, record his comments in your notes, complete with bells and whistles.

If your professor doesn't mention any outside publications, do some research yourself to find out what he has written. A good place to start is your law school catalog, which will probably list—with pride—each professor's principal publications. Or consult the library's index of publications. However, keep in mind that you will be tested on what is in the textbook and what is covered in class—don't spend all your time reading a professor's outside publications and ignore what is actually happening in class.

Repetition

When a professor repeats an idea, a phrase, or (most importantly) a definition, write it down. Repetition indicates that the professor considers the information important.

Material Discussed in the Last Two Weeks of Class

Keep your "ears peeled" during the last two weeks of class. Even if your professor is covering new material, she will give clues about the exam. One way or another, most teachers refer to much of the material that they intend to test.

For example, you may notice that your professor mentions, in April, a principle you covered in January. Since April is exam-preparation time, your professor probably mentioned the topic in class because she has just made it part of an exam question.

Physical Cues

Professors often give nonverbal clues of what's likely to appear on their exams.

Key Points Are Most Often Given During the Opening and Closing Minutes of Class

Research indicates that professors are most likely to mention important points during the first and last few minutes of class; therefore, it's very important to arrive early and get yourself settled before the professor starts speaking, and to keep taking notes until he finishes. If you start packing up while the professor is still talking, you may well miss the most important point made during class. You may be lucky enough to have a professor who summarizes what you were supposed to learn.

Write Down Anything Your Professor Writes on the Board

If your professor takes the time to write something on the board, she is signaling that she considers it to be important. Given that fact, you may want to indicate in your notes that an item appeared on the board. You can do this by enclosing the item in a box, or by marking it with a distinguishing symbol.

Note When Your Professor Is Excited About Something

If a professor seems more animated than usual, his animation probably indicates that he is particularly interested in the topic, and that it may well appear on the exam. Try to notice any changes in a professor's delivery style: a new inflection, a raised voice, a slower speed of speaking. Once you learn to recognize your professor's individual style, any noticeable variation can signal that the information being discussed is important.

Watch the Professor's Eyes

When the professor glances at her lecture notes and then makes a point, that point is probably important. Material recorded in her notes is likely to show up on the exam; after all, she will probably prepare the exam from these notes.

Things that Can Interfere with Taking Good Notes

Don't Allow Your Prejudices to Influence Your Perceptions

Occasionally, you'll cover material in class that upsets you. For example, you may violently disagree with the insanity defense. Or, perhaps you were once involved in a lawsuit over an auto accident, and any discussion of contributory negligence makes your blood boil. Or, your professor may be a fascist, a racist, or a sexist, and you're furious over some of the things he says. Whatever your attitude, you can't afford to conduct an internal dialogue during class. If you do so, it will interfere with your ability to absorb new information, which is the whole purpose of attending class. If you have to clear your head, write your thoughts down quickly, then turn back to the discussion in class. Postpone any internal debate or turmoil until class is over. For note-taking purposes, keep in mind that it's okay to take down information you don't personally agree with. After all, every legal dispute has at least two possible resolutions. Look at taking notes as a game that you win only by figuring out what will be on the exam. Most importantly, don't upset yourself by taking anything that transpires in class as a personal affront.

Don't Panic if You Get Lost

Everyone gets lost at times in the class discussion. If you lose your focus, just put some kind of "lost" signal in your notes (perhaps a double question mark) and leave some space to be filled in later. Remember, you're taking notes for subsequent review. Writing down an "I'm lost" signal will remind you that you missed something, and, if you can't figure it out yourself after class, you can check with someone else about it or refer to a commercial study aid. Resolving confusion in this way will allow you to regain your focus, instead of continuing to worry about what you missed.

Avoid Goofing Off On Your Computer

Shut down all Web sites, games, and instant-messaging or e-mail programs.

What if the Professor Is Putting You to Sleep?

Boring law professors are, unfortunately, not terribly rare. Try as you may to follow the class, occasionally you may find it an unbearable burden. To reinvigorate yourself, try a simple "oxygenating" exercise.

❶ Straighten up. Sit as though a string at the top of your head is holding you up like a marionette. Put your feet on the floor and uncross your arms and legs.

❷ Take a deep breath and hold it.

❸ Tense all your muscles from the ground up. Start with your feet, and move up from your legs to your torso, shoulders, neck, jaw, forehead, upper and lower arms, and hands. Keep each muscle tense for five seconds, and then relax.

❹ Take another deep, slow breath, using all your stomach and chest muscles. Pause for a moment, and then exhale completely. When you've exhaled as much as you think you can, force out even more air by contracting your stomach muscles and rounding your lips. Repeat this breathing pattern two more times.

❺ Take another deep breath, hold it, tense all your muscles again (as described above), hold for five seconds, and relax.

With practice, you'll find that you can do this in class without calling undue attention to yourself. The same maneuvers will revive you if you feel sleepy when studying.

Traps to Avoid When Taking Notes

This book has already referred to a few traps: writing too much or too little and doodling over your notes themselves. Here are others to avoid.

Tape Recording the Lectures

If you are present in class, your tape recorder shouldn't be. Students who record lectures are often viewed as zealous, but recording lectures can actually hinder your learning. There are two reasons for this:

Recording a Lecture Tends to Make You Relax Mentally

One of the basic tenets of this book is that, to be effective, your efforts at learning must be active, not passive. You may believe that recording a lecture will allow you to concentrate on it more fully than if you take notes. This isn't true. Taping a lecture merely allows your mind to drift off; taking good notes does not. And ask yourself: What can I get out of the tapes later that I can't get now, especially if I concentrate and take good notes?

You'll Never Listen to the Tape

Believing that you'll listen to tapes of lectures you've already sat through is like believing you'll read those two-year-old copies of the *Wall Street Journal* stored in your attic; it may happen, but it's unlikely. In any case, if you take the kind of notes discussed above, listening to taped lectures is a waste of time, and this book's primary goal is to make you a top student while saving you time.

You Hesitate to Ask a Question Because You Think You'll Be Embarrassed

At some point, you'll probably want to ask a question in class, but you won't because you're afraid of looking stupid. This happens to every student. When it happens to you, write the question down and save it for after class.

No one can avoid having an occasional question that she is too embarrassed to ask. Professors advise students to go ahead and ask their question anyway because if they haven't "got it," other students haven't either. The problem with this advice in law school is that law school classes are intimidating at the best of times; the thought of putting your self-esteem at the mercy of a law professor is downright unappealing, and it's often unnecessary.

So why not save the question until after class? Most professors are willing to stay after class for a few minutes to answer students' questions. Knowing that you can ask questions after class has an additional benefit: It will save you from wasting time worrying about whether to raise your hand. Instead, you'll devote your class time to paying attention to the discussion and taking good notes. If you save your question until after class, and it proves to be a good one, the worst that can happen is that your professor will say, "That's a good question. I wish you'd asked it in class." That may increase your willingness to offer your questions more easily in later sessions with that professor.

Practice Taking Good Notes

You may have spent a lifetime taking poor notes. If so, you may be concerned about your ability to develop a better system and fear you'll miss something in class that you'll never be able to retrieve. Tackle your fear first and head-on. You can easily practice note-taking in a non-law-school environment, with the added benefit of becoming well-informed in the process. It's simple—practice taking notes of the TV news. Watch the news with a pen and paper at your side and take notes about the news, just as you would for a class. During commercials, review your notes and revise them. When the news is over, spend five minutes reviewing your notes.

This practice has two advantages:

❶ It will train you to listen for key points; and

❷ it will teach you to focus your attention on what's being said, even when the topic may not interest you.

Remember: You need do this only if you feel insecure about your note-taking skills.

If Your Professor Is an Incoherent Babbler

Law professors are neither demons nor gods. Some law professors take to teaching after many years of practice as lawyers, when they realize that their productive working days are over. Other lawyers enter the teaching profession to find a "safe haven" after unsuccessful efforts to make it in the law. These professors may not like students or know how to deal with them. What's more, they may not have any notion of how to teach.

Unfortunately, almost every law school has at least one professor like this, and you could end up stuck with him. If so, you may find yourself sitting in class, listening intently and wondering what on earth he is talking about. One student reported the experience of listening to an elderly professor spend an entire class session discoursing on why old men should have their flies sewn shut. Upperclassmen at your school may recount similar stories about your professors. In almost every case, other professors are well aware that they have an incompetent in their midst. It's just a fact of life. Take comfort in knowing that others around you appreciate and share your dilemma.

Unfortunately, if you have a professor like this, you won't be able to implement the advice in this chapter because you won't glean anything from class that's worth writing down. If you find yourself in this situation, you'll have to rely on other tactics. For example, analyzing old exams will become even more important for you than with other professors. You can also ask upperclass students how they handled this professor; what did they do to compensate for the lack of good class notes? If these sources aren't available—if, for example, the professor has just joined the faculty—resign yourself to teaching yourself the material. Read a hornbook, listen to a CD or an audiotape on the subject, and use the best commercial outline you can find in order to get a handle on the subject. Go to your school's academic support professional and see if she has any insight on how to handle the class. In addition, ask your professor point blank what you're expected to know for the exam. Don't settle for generalities; you'll need specifics in order to prepare. If you do all this, you can be sure, at the very least, that others in the class have no better chance than you of doing well.

The Classroom Experience
The Socratic Method

Have you ever heard inflicting humiliation characterized as an effective learning tool? When you were learning to read, did your parents hand you the *Wall Street Journal* and then laugh at you when you couldn't read or understand it? Did they grill you about it in front of your friends? Not likely. Unfortunately, an analogous device—the Socratic method—is the predominant method of teaching law. The Socratic method is teaching through questioning and is intended to develop your legal reasoning abilities. In theory, a professor who teaches by the Socratic method will never actually explain anything to you. Instead, she will ask questions supposedly designed to help you discover the facts and principles of each case by yourself. A typical Socratic exchange may go something like this:

PROFESSOR: Ms. Student, what did the uncle write to the nephew?
STUDENT: The uncle promised to pay the nephew $5,000 if the nephew behaved.
PROFESSOR: Great—so you know how to read at least. I'm never sure with law students. So, did the nephew give the uncle anything in return?
STUDENT: No.
PROFESSOR: Really? Are you sure? Did the uncle receive any benefit from the arrangement? Nothing? Nothing at all?
STUDENT: Not really, other than the benefit of having a well-behaved nephew.
PROFESSOR: Well, that certainly sounds fantastic! That's worth its weight in gold! Must the uncle receive a benefit from the nephew in order for his promise to be enforceable?

And so on until the student articulates the rule (in this case) of consideration. You can see how embarrassing the above exchange could be if you had not adequately briefed the case and had no idea what uncle the professor was talking about. Also, if you have not prepared for class, you will not be aware that consideration is today's topic and you won't know where the professor's questions are heading. In practice, the Socratic method often results in a professor (who has spent *years* studying, reading about, and analyzing a subject) making you (who have spent a few days studying the material) look foolish. When you think about it, you begin to understand the process—it's precisely because she does know the subject so well that the professor is able to make you look so foolish.

Judged as a teaching technique, the Socratic method does not always seem a particularly effective means of imparting a lawyer's skills or knowledge. Classes taught this way rarely reach firm conclusions about legal principles, even though these principles are, essentially, what you will need to apply on your exams. A professor who teaches this way may never even mention what the conclusion of a discussion is; she may just move on to the next case, leaving you to draw your own conclusions.

One argument often used to defend the Socratic method is that professors must use it because those students who plan to practice before appellate courts will eventually face the same kind of grilling from judges. This hardly seems an adequate justification for subjecting *every* student to the humiliation the Socratic method involves; few lawyers become involved in appellate practice. It can be argued that if law schools really wanted to develop skills that many students will eventually need, they would teach commonly used legal forms, the art of interviewing a witness, and general office administration.

However, you'll eventually come to realize that there is a great deal of merit in the Socratic method. It does teach you how to recognize and break down the primary facts you have to deal with in any given situation, to apply to these facts a process of analysis that forces you to consider every possible approach and solution, to consider as well the weapons of your adversary, and then to form your conclusions and a precise course of action.

In takes awhile, however, to recognize these benefits. In the meantime, the immediate results of the Socratic method are rampant humiliation, panic, and embarrassment among students. But these feelings can be dealt with—more or less.

Dealing with the Humiliation

First, identify the source of your professor's power: Not only does he have superior knowledge of the subject matter, he is the one asking the questions; if he wishes, he can adjust the questioning to your responses, shifting perspectives in order to force you into a corner (in fact, even if the professor was asking you questions about *yourself*, he could eventually ask you a question you don't know the answer to). The nature of the law gives the professor the edge. As you know, law is a continuum—the answer to any issue lies in where you draw the line between what is reasonable and what is not. Your professor can quickly force you into attempting to defend an indefensible position simply by making you justify any line you draw. Remember, many legal rules are intended to serve merely as guidelines, and depend entirely on the facts of a particular case; they may not be theoretically defensible when applied to changed circumstances or facts. In fact, many of the cases in your casebook were "wrongly" decided; the court may have come to the wrong conclusion or reasoned illogically. When a professor forces you to defend yourself, he knows in advance that you won't "win" the argument; you're not supposed to. If you accept that fact ahead of time, you'll be more relaxed, and the exchange with the professor will be less painful.

When you're called on in class, take a long, deep breath, put down your pen, and listen carefully to what is asked of you; then, plunge in. Give it your best shot and ignore (to the extent possible) the fact that everyone is paying attention to you. Remember, everyone in class will be grilled at some point; you won't think badly of your classmates, as long as they *are prepared* and make a decent effort to respond. In the same way, they won't think less of you if you don't sound like Oliver Wendell Holmes (nobody does). If you find some professors particularly intimidating, try the simple trick of imagining that they're students just like you. (They were at one time.) This should help you overcome your anxiety, since your fellow students are not apt to be intimidating to you after you hear a few of them respond in class.

Suppose your worst nightmare comes true: You make a supremely boneheaded statement in class. Perhaps you define negligence as an intentional act, or you define *obiter dicta* as statements in a decision important to the holding; or, worst of all, you defend some principle with mighty arguments that are shattered by your professor with one deft statement. The professor can make you look extremely foolish. How should you handle it?

First, realize what has actually happened: All you've done is make one silly statement, and *making* a single silly statement in a class you're taking for the first time doesn't mean that you're stupid. You shouldn't allow anything that happens in class to affect your belief that you can succeed in law school. Nothing can diminish your innate ability if you don't let it. In Chapter 2, The Mind-Set of Success, this book emphasized that you could flub every question all year long and still get great grades because your grades depend solely on your exams. The way people sound in class has nothing to do with their class rank at the end of the year. Some people are just better at instant reasoning and quick repartee.

That doesn't mean they'll get better grades or be better lawyers. Brilliant performance in class is only one indication that a student may do well on exams. Similarly, the converse is simply not true—a poor showing in class has no bearing on how well a person will do on an exam. If you perform poorly in class, accept it as a temporary setback and then forget it.

Class Participation

Every law school class has at least one student who feels she must air her brilliance in every discussion. You shouldn't be intimidated by these people. But should *you* make an effort to take part in class discussions?

The party line from law school professors is that you should actively participate in class discussions because participation enhances your law school experience. This book's advice is quite different: Volunteer in class only if you feel comfortable doing so. Your sole purpose is to get superior grades. While frequent class participation may have a slight "extra-credit" effect, many people get top grades without ever volunteering in class. In fact, since most exams are graded anonymously, who you are and what you said in class will have no bearing on how your professor evaluates the exam. If raising your hand makes you uncomfortable, don't do it. What's more, don't feel guilty about not doing it! Taking part in a heated class discussion may even harm your performance; if you're too involved, you may miss some "cues" your professor has given.

Of course, you should participate if you really like to discuss things in class (and participating can help keep you awake). You may want to be careful, though, to avoid talking so excessively that you alienate your classmates. After all, you never know when you'll need someone's notes or help, and if you alienate others by sounding pompous or being excessively aggressive, they won't be anxious to help you out. Try to remember that what you say in class is your opinion and nothing more, and that everyone else in class has an opinion on the same issue, even if he keeps it to himself.

Chapter 6
Outlining

The Function of Outlining

The challenge in outlining lies in organizing your class notes into a hierarchical structure that will help you on your exams. If you've taken your notes as suggested in the note-taking chapter, the process of outlining will be relatively easy—simply a matter of condensing and organizing those notes, along with any information from secondary sources, into a structure of headings, subheadings, and sub-subheadings, each followed by a short note or summary. If you outline successfully, you will improve your exam results enormously.

There are two principal benefits to outlining:

❶ cementing information in your mind and helping you see the overall structure of the course, and

❷ providing the "external storage" function, by which you create a reference document that's convenient to use later.

The first benefit is the more important one; to derive this benefit, it's essential that you prepare the outline yourself. What you include will reflect your organization of the course materials in a way that is meaningful to you. Every word in the outline should act as a cue for its source— your class notes, a case, or a secondary source. Your outline will be unique to you. Someone else's outline will never be quite as useful, although it may help to clarify any points you don't understand.

The following example illustrates how outlining can fit into your overall approach to study. Assume you're assigned the case of *Fisher v. Carrousel Motor Hotel,* 424 S.W.2d 627 (Tex. 1967) for your Torts class. In this case, Defendant "makes contact" with Plaintiff by snatching a plate from his hands; he never actually touches the Plaintiff. You'd begin by reading (carefully) and briefing the case, including sufficient detail about the facts, holding, and rationale to allow you to understand the case and to talk about it in class. If you were outlining, you would limit the level of detail. You'd condense the case down to the basic facts and a basic rule and then incorporate that rule into your outline. Make sure you use a traditional outline format when making your outline. (Most computer word-processing programs can do the formatting for you.) It is a classic mistake for first-year law students to simply recopy their notes or list one case after another. If you do your outline that way, it will be useless to you.

You might create the basic heading "Battery." Under the subheading, "Contact Required for Battery," you'd write, "definition satisfied by contact with anything attached to plaintiff's body and practically identified with it." When you begin preparing for your exam, you'd study this rule as part of your study of battery ("contact" is one of the elements of battery).

Often, it helps to create and memorize a mnemonic—a memory aid—to help your recall of rules that have several components. The specific holding of *Fisher v. Carrousel* would not form an explicit mnemonic by itself. Instead, you'd place it into a more inclusive mnemonic of all the elements of battery. This would help you to recall that the "contact" element of battery doesn't require that the plaintiff himself be "touched."

Creating an Outline

The type of outline you create will depend on whether your exam is open or closed book. Both types of exam require that you memorize your outline; the principal difference between the two lies in what your professor will expect in your answer. (This book will discuss open- versus closed-book exams in Chapter 8, Test-Taking.) If you don't know what kind of exam it will be, it's best to assume that it will be a closed-book exam. When creating your outline, keep your exams in mind (e.g., you won't be writing a full-page explanation of the facts of an underlying case in your exam answer; at most, you might write one or two sentences). In many ways, if you create your outline correctly, you'll be "pre-writing" your exam answers.

When to Outline

As a rule of thumb, you should start outlining about two or three weeks into the semester (as soon as you have covered enough information in class that you can outline it). To get the most out of your outline, you should continually update, revise, and memorize it as you go through the semester. Additionally, you should work on the outline for *every* class weekly. Often, students will take a week or two to outline Torts, and then a week or two to outline Criminal Law, and so on until exams begin. However, the problem with this strategy is that by the time exams have come around, you haven't looked at

Torts for several weeks and whatever class you've waited until the end to outline will likely be rushed as exams get closer.

If you've been studying by "progressive parts," it won't take you very long to outline each course. Your outlines should be complete early in your reading period—the time after classes finish and before exams start. If you finish your outlines early, use the remaining time for review. Brushing up on points that give you trouble and practicing with questions from old exams are the most useful way to spend your time.

Creating an Outline for a Closed-Book Exam

Most of your exams are likely to be closed book. To create an outline for a closed-book exam, continue with what you've been doing all along: going from a "macro" view of the course to a "micro" view of the course. As long as you've kept up with condensing your notes onto note cards (or in some other way), outlining involves simply condensing the material even further.

Format

Many students use the table of contents from their casebook or their course syllabus as the skeleton for their outline. One of the best tools is to follow—although you may have to modify it to conform to your own course—the table of contents of a good commercial outline. If you choose this method, for each topic, you should include

- ❶ the principal rule(s) in the field,
- ❷ the rationale for the rule(s),
- ❸ any major exceptions to the rule(s), and
- ❹ condensed examples drawn from the professor's hypotheticals and the cases you've covered.

An Example

This could be a skeletal outline of major headings for a typical Torts course:

1. Intentional torts: intended interference with the person
2. Intentional torts: intentional interference with property
3. Negligent torts

4. Damages
5. Vicarious liability
6. Proximate cause
7. Duty
8. Defenses
9. Joint tortfeasors
10. Strict liability
11. Misrepresentation
12. Defamation
13. Product liability

In your outline, you'd add subheadings and sub-subheadings in each section of the "skeleton" by condensing material from your notes. Build your outline around the black-letter-law rule for each subject. This is how part of the first section of your outline might look:

I. Intentional Torts: Interference with the Person
    A. BATTERY—unpermitted and harmful or offensive touching of another by an act intended to result in such contact. Interest protected is bodily integrity, not injury to body.
        1. "Touching"—need not touch person, but anything "practically attached to or identified with" him. *Fisher v. Carrousel (grabbing plate).*
        2. Intent—if actor desired to bring it about or knew with substantial certainty that it would occur as a result of his action. *Garratt v. Dailey (5-year-old boy pulling chair out from under woman).* Malice not required. What one knows says a lot about what one intends.
            a. Transferred Intent—intend to hit someone, but hit someone else. *Talmadge v. Smith (person throws stick at one person, hits another).*
        3. Damages—can recover physical and mental damages flowing proximately from that contact.
        4. Defenses
            a. Consent is a complete defense to battery.
                1. Express—actual consent by plaintiff.

    2.   Implied—by actions, plaintiff permits "person" to be interfered with (for example, agreeing to play touch football). Also, people must put up with a certain amount of touching in society (for example, jostling on a subway).

   b.   Privilege—limited, allowing proportionate response in the circumstances (but liable if person goes beyond that).

Features of Good Outlines

Outlines Are Idiosyncratic

If you followed the above outline closely, you may have thought, "I would have worded that differently" or "I wouldn't have included those examples." That's fine. This sample outline reflects only what one particular student might have gleaned from cases she read and from the ideas her professor emphasized. If you look closely, you can almost see the thought process by which she reduced her class notes and briefs to note cards and then incorporated only the bare essentials into her outline. Every line of her outline is intended to trigger her own memory, to help her recall the material from which it was condensed.

Sparse Mention of Case Names

Usually, exact case names are not important to high grades on exams (unless your professor specifically requires you to include them), so why include them at all? The reason is that some students have the ability to associate the case name easily with the rule or principle it stands for. The name acts as a cue to the rule, and vice versa. It functions in the same way as the title to a song. Recall the title, and you will remember the lyrics, or the wonderful person you were with the first time you heard it.

The Incorporation of Reasons and Conclusions

Note that the above outline of Battery recites the reasons to allow recovery and the personal interests that the tort affects—in other words, the reason and the public policy goal behind the definition of Battery. It's vital that you remember the reason and purpose behind each rule because exam questions are unlikely to mirror exactly any case or hypothetical you've covered in class. Exam questions tend to explore areas that "fall between the cracks" of the facts you've learned; therefore, you have to remember not only the rule itself, but also the reason behind it. In that way, you can apply the reason to any new sets of facts on your professor's exam and arrive at a conclusion you can justify. (This will be discussed in more detail in Chapter 7, Test Preparation, and Chapter 8, Test-Taking.)

Focus on the "Forest" Rather than the "Trees"

Note also that the outline doesn't dwell on any single detail of Battery; instead, it states, in a very basic way, all the essential aspects of the tort. Definitions, rationales, and examples are brief and to the point. If you had to refer to the outline during an exam, you'd be able to locate any important point quickly and easily.

Don't Spend Time on the History of Each Concept

Textbooks include substantial sections discussing the historical evolution of the legal principles you're dealing with. While these sections may help you to understand the principles, and the rationales and policies behind them, they won't get you any points on an exam, so you needn't refer to them in your outline. The history is important to you only to the extent that it points to the reason for the rule.

The Use of Secondary Sources

Although the sample outline doesn't include them, there's nothing wrong with incorporating elements from secondary sources into your outline. For instance, if you find the hypotheticals or analysis from another source particularly useful, include them. Be careful, though, not to go beyond the scope of your course. For instance, if your Torts professor didn't cover trade disparagement, don't study it, even if every study aid mentions it. It can't be on your exam if it's not covered in class, so it shouldn't be in your outline.

How Long Should I Make My Outline?

If you're a typical law student and love to argue or debate, try asking people how long they think outlines should be. You'll find more division of opinion on this topic than on any other study issue. Some professors believe you should be able to condense an entire course into a one-page outline; others say no outline should be longer than a dozen pages. In this case, you should take the advice of Abraham Lincoln. Lincoln said that a person's legs should be long enough to reach from his body to the ground. In the same way, an outline should be long enough to do the job *you need it to do*—to cover the course.

Remember, your outline is only one link in your chain of preparation, which starts with reading cases and will finish with your final exam preparation. As you condense your notes and then convert them into an outline, using the format suggested, your outline will end up no longer or shorter than it needs to be. Once you've condensed your notes into an outline format, the next step will be to create mnemonic devices to reduce the essential information even further. (This is covered in Chapter 7, Test Preparation.) Don't leave out material facts just to fit your outline into an arbitrary number of pages. If it takes you 50 pages to get the absolute basics of the course into your outline, then your outline should be 50 pages long. (By the way, that was the total length of the outline the above sample came from.) It's better to have a complete overview of all the material principles in the class than to leave out essentials—such as rationales or examples—just to shorten your outline.

Creating an Outline for an Open-Book Exam

Surprisingly, you'll have to do the same amount of memorizing for an open-book exam as for a closed-book exam. If your exam is open book, your professor will be looking for more analysis and issue-spotting skills than she would with a closed-book exam. Also, your professor will expect you to state rules *correctly,* since she will assume you have them in front of you (in your outline). Consequently, you have to know the material *very* well. You may not have time to leaf through your outline for every answer. Importantly, you'll need to study for an open-book exam just as much as for a closed-book exam. (Don't get lulled into a false sense of security.)

Here are some tips for creating a useful outline for an open-book exam:

Index, Index, Index

Many students find that indexing is the key to a successful outline for an open-book exam. Perhaps the most valuable investment you can make for your outline is stick-on tabs or labels that you can attach to the edge of your pages. You can mark these with the main topic on each page. The tabs will enable you to go quickly from one topic to another.

Table of Contents

A table of contents can be another helpful resource for your outline. When you have completed your final outline, simply paginate it and note the page numbers of main topic headings. Then put the headings into alphabetical order (or whatever order makes sense to you) and form the table of contents for your outline.

Macro- vs. Micro-Outlines

During an open-book exam, you'll want the following tools close at hand:

✎ An "Issue Checklist" Covering the Course

What's an issue checklist, you ask? It's a summary of all the issues you might be confronted with on an exam. Your issue checklist may resemble your skeleton outline addressing the major topics covered in class. Or it may look more like this sample from a Contracts exam checklist:

> Is there a valid contract?
>   If so, was the contract satisfied?
>   If not, are there grounds for reformation or rescission?
> Is there a breach?
> What are the defenses?

If you run each exam question through your checklist, you'll spot most, if not all, of the issues raised by the question. On an open-book exam, you can prepare the checklist in advance and take it with you. On a closed-book exam, you need to commit the issue checklist to memory and jot it down as the first thing you do in your exam.

✎ A Bare Bones, "Macro-Outline" of the Course

The outline shown above for the tort of Battery is a macro, "bare-bones" outline, one that includes the *basics* on every major topic in the course. You can affix the sticky notes directly to the pages of this outline. When you write the outline, you may choose to refer to related points in your text, notes, or briefs, in case you want to review a specific point in more detail for the exam. For example, you could utilize abbreviations like "t" for text, "n" for notes, and "b" for briefs; then, next to each element of your "bare-bones" outline, you could include a reference, such as "t-21" or "n-11," to tell you where in your notes or other source you can find a fuller explanation of the principle or example.

Even if you prepare and bring a micro-outline (see below) to your exam, you may still want to add a macro-outline to your materials. Using your issue checklist, you can decide which topic heading you are seeking and then turn to that section in your macro-outline. If your memory still isn't sufficiently jogged, you have your micro-outline available and cross-referenced. This may seem like a lot of paperwork for one exam, but whatever it takes to increase your grade will be well worth the extra minutes in preparation.

✎ A "Micro-Outline" of the Course

A micro-outline is a more extensive outline that includes your case briefs and class notes, which you may or may not choose to index. You should, if you can, reduce your "micro" outline to a "macro" outline before the exam. Getting the longer one down to the shorter one will force you to conduct a thorough review of the whole subject. If you've created an effective macro-outline, you shouldn't need to look at this "micro-outline" very often. The point is that the elements of the macro-outline should trigger in your mind the details of the more extensive micro-outline. In any case, you'll probably be too rushed during the exam to spend time hunting through pages and pages of briefs and notes. If you're well-prepared, that won't be necessary in any case. Even though you're unlikely to use the more extended outline during the exam, you may still choose to have it with you; it may function as a "security blanket" because you know the material is there if you really need it.

CHAPTER 7
Test Preparation

You're finally in the home stretch! If you've been diligent about your studies and have continually reviewed and organized your class materials, victory is at hand. On the other hand, if you haven't been as diligent as you might have been, now is the time to catch up. This chapter will discuss how to maximize the effectiveness of your final review.

Test preparation is the penultimate step in this book's seven-step approach to getting great grades. Outlining was the final step in creating your study materials; now, during the test preparation stage, you'll begin to make the best use of those materials. Your test preparation will require you to practice the skills that make for good exam performance: understanding, remembering, and applying the law.

As with every other element in this approach, your review must be active. Active review shortens your prep time and gives you the feedback you need to evaluate your progress. As you prepare for your finals, it's critical to gauge exactly how much you know because it's your last chance to fill in gaps. At this stage in your learning, your job should consist of memorizing your outline (in its briefest possible form), as well as asking yourself possible exam questions and writing down practice answers. This chapter will discuss both elements in detail, along with "external" factors that can influence the effectiveness of your study sessions.

Where to Study

Choosing the correct "environment" in which to study will make remembering legal principles easier for you. You'll want to take advantage of the best study location and avoid any possible interference ("interference" will be discussed later, in the section, "Memorization Techniques").

The Room Where You Study Can Affect Your Memory

Research has shown that when you learn something in a particular environment you'll recall it more easily in that environment than anywhere else. Parts of the environment become cues for your memory because they become associated with the material you learned there. If possible, try to study in the very room in which you'll be tested (or in a similar classroom). If this simply isn't possible, you can still use environment to help you. Often, if you have difficulty remembering, forcing yourself to recall details about the room in which you did study the point in question will help to jog your memory. If you don't know where your exam will be, or if you can't study there, it may be helpful to practice studying in several different locations. That way, the content of your material will assume a life of its own, independent of time and place.

Study Without Distractions

To study effectively, you should avoid distractions. If you must have noise in the background, try music without words, a quiet fan, or an aquarium. If you are forced to study in a noisy location, carry an MP3 player and listen to soft instrumental music that won't distract you.

Study in Bright Light

If possible, study in natural light. When this isn't possible, make sure the artificial light is as bright as can be. Studying is at best an arduous process and it depresses many people. Bright light reduces depression; darkness increases it.

If You Have a Tendency to Panic, Avoid Other Panickers

Misery may love company, but it definitely doesn't help your studies to surround yourself with other students who are nervous about the upcoming exam. Actually, except for help in batting around hypothetical questions and answers, you can't really get any help from others in the last days before an exam. You're better off all by yourself in some quiet corner.

Adjust Your Wake-Up Time, If Necessary

To ensure peak performance on your exam, you need to be mentally alert when the exam begins. If you're scheduled to take an exam at 9:00 a.m. but you aren't accustomed to waking up early, you should adjust your wake-up time at least a week in advance of the exam. Force yourself to get up every day at the same time you'll need to in order to be ready on the day of the exam. Eat a good breakfast and don't rush.

Attend Any Special Exam-Preparation Sessions Offered by Your Professors or Academic Support Program

Make sure you attend any special exam-preparation sessions offered by your professor or your school's academic support professional, and take advantage of any other help offered.

While this advice may strike you as obvious and gratuitous, it's amazing how many students believe their study time is better spent reviewing their own notes than attending these sessions. At review sessions, listen closely for any clues the professor may give about the contents of the exam. Also, if you have any questions about exam coverage or format, this is the opportunity to clear them up.

As suggested earlier, you should also pay special attention to what your professor says during the last two weeks of class. Even if he is covering new material, he will give you clues about the exam; many professors refer, in some way, to most of the topics that will be tested. Listen especially for reviews or references to topics covered early in the semester because they may well appear on the exam.

If your school's academic support program holds simulated or practice exams, make sure you attend them (and take them seriously). These sessions can provide you with valuable practice and help you discover weak spots in your exam preparation.

Study Sessions

Optimum Length of Study Sessions

Don't study for more than one-and-a-half hours without a break. Ideally, you should study for about 45 minutes, relax for 10 or 15 minutes, and then go back to studying. Breaks are vital to effective studying. They give you a chance to think about and digest what you've studied. Also, a 45-minute study "bite" supports an organized and disciplined view of a topic or rule. If you don't take breaks, you'll quickly "overload" and lose the sense of organization that's so vital to good study results. Any benefit gained from longer study sessions will be minimal.

During the 15 minute break, do something else. Get something to eat or drink, pick up a novel or newspaper, take a walk, talk to some friends, or simply move around.

Avoid Studying Different Subjects

If possible, don't study more than one subject during a study session. Even if your sessions are separated only by your getting a drink of water or by leaving the room for a few minutes and then returning, the concentration on one subject per session will reduce "concept interference" between the subjects. If you must study more than one subject during a single study session, make sure the subjects aren't similar in their basic concepts. For example, don't study Criminal Law and Torts together, or you may confuse the two.

The Content of Study Sessions

Some things to keep in mind during your study sessions.

Serial Position Effect

Because of what's called the "serial-position effect," items that appear in the middle of a list or outline take longer to learn and are harder to remember than material at the beginning or the end. Keeping this in mind, make sure that you study the more difficult, less comprehensible items at the beginning and end of each study session (and the easier-to-learn, more obvious items in the middle). For instance, if you find landlord/tenant and adverse possession to be simple Property concepts, but you find conveyancing to be difficult, study conveyancing at the beginning and/or end of your study session and landlord/tenant and adverse possession in the middle. It you can't rearrange the order of the items you have to study, then you should allocate more time to the difficult items than to the easy ones. Or you may want to spend one entire session on a difficult item, for instance, conveyancing, and possibly go back to it a second or third time. These practices should help you avoid the serial-position effect.

Readjust Your Focus in the Last Days Before the Exam

A few days before your test, you should identify and focus on the items you suspect you don't know. Many students fall into a trap—they spend their review time repeatedly going over material they know well and ignoring parts they don't know. A simple way to find out what you don't know is to go through a commercial outline or study aid. Put aside the information you can answer easily and focus on the information with which you have some trouble. Reviewing this way again and again will eventually move all topics into the category of material you know well.

Some Traps to Avoid

When Material Starts to Look Familiar, Don't Fall into the Trap of Thinking You Know It

Many students study by simply scanning their notes and texts and assuming that the underlying material has sunk in. This is not a good way to study for law school exams; your exams won't test recognition, they'll test analysis of underlying principles. To do well, you need to take an active role—asking questions to test your ability to analyze, using review aids, and memorizing the material.

Don't Spend Time on Unimportant Details

If you're a perfectionist (or think law school requires that you become one), you may be tempted to spend your study time on some extremely difficult, obtuse concept. You'll take pride in mastering something no one else seems to think important. Sure, if it's on the exam, you'll "blow it out of the water," but if it's not likely to be on the exam, your diligence will be wasted.

If you spend your time this way, you'll neglect the very issues that will almost certainly appear on your exam. You'll be less prepared to discuss the issues your professor is thinking about. If you must be perfect in all things, be especially careful as you prepare for exams. You may lose focus and become bogged down in unimportant details. For example, if you find yourself reading law review articles, you're wasting valuable study time. Law review articles, by their very nature, don't look at "the big picture"; they typically involve a detailed analysis of a very specific and often esoteric point of law. During your test preparation, give up trying to master every obscure theory and detail in the course. Take pride instead in mastering the *major* concepts.

Don't bury yourself in details.

Simulating Exams

While memorizing your outline and reviewing flashcards, you should practice two other valuable exercises during your test preparation: Simulate the exam using questions from past exams (if available) and make up your own exam questions.

When you do these exercises, it will help if you compare your notes with the notes of others (e.g., the other students in your study group, or a group of your friends). Each of you can practice answering questions the others make up. And you can each offer comments, suggestions, and criticism of each answer, helping the student submitting the answer to recognize the points on which she needs to spend additional time.

Questions from Old Exams

Answering old exam questions can have a significant and positive impact on your grades, so you should practice with them whenever they're available and take your practice very seriously. Professors tend to repeat themselves, and an old exam can be a preview of your exam. In addition, there are many study aids that are designed specifically to offer help and practice with questions and answers. The more you use them, the more skill and experience you will acquire in relating facts to issues; recognizing and analyzing issues; and writing clear, cogent, and intelligent answers.

The following are a few pointers about tools in exam preparation.

Simulate Exam Conditions

When you practice with old exams, take the exams in an environment as similar as possible to that of your actual exam. If you can sit in the classroom where you will be taking the actual exam, terrific. Otherwise, make sure you simulate other exam conditions, such as controlling your time, so you'll know what to expect when you face the "real thing." Poor time management skills are the downfall of many students, and practicing with old exams under time pressure is the best way to improve those skills. Read Chapter 8, Test-Taking, before practicing with old exam questions, and follow the procedures outlined there. If you don't want to practice taking an entire exam at once, follow the procedures for working with individual questions.

Review the Professor's Exam Questions

When you answer old questions, study the questions themselves to see what they tell you about the things your professor is likely to test and they way she organizes her exams. Ask yourself: Based on the exam questions, what does the professor seem to consider important? What's the main thrust of each question? Does the professor emphasize trivial facts, or does she stick to the broad principles? Are the fact patterns complex, or is the emphasis on analysis and exposition? Are the situations presented concrete or abstract? To what extent (if any) does she test on things she didn't cover in class? (For instance, if she rushed through material at the end of the semester, does she nevertheless emphasize it on the exam to make sure you understand it?) Remember, while your professor is unlikely to repeat a specific question from last year's exam, the person who wrote that exam is the same as the one creating this year's, so the two exams will probably be substantially similar in organization, form, and concept, if not in their details.

Go Back Several Years, if the Exams Are Available

While your professor's recent exams will teach you the professor's exam techniques, he will almost certainly vary the questions considerably from year to year. However, he may occasionally reuse or rephrase an exam question from an older exam. Your professor may assume that you will look at last year's exam, but won't bother to look up exams that are older. Take advantage of that assumption. Review at least five years of old exams, if they're available. After a while, you'll begin to see a pattern that will define the items you need to develop and concentrate on.

Chart Questions Over the Last Few Years

By this time, you should have prepared your outline of the major topics covered in your class. Now, make a chart. List the five past years across the top and the major topics down the left-hand side. Then, note under each year which of the major topics appeared that year on your professor's exam. If you see a major topic on the exam that's not on your own list, by all means add it and ask

yourself why you missed it. The chart will help you predict what issues are likely to appear on this year's exam. (If an issue appears every year on your chart, the professor will be likely to include it on this year's exam. On the other hand, if she is careful to vary the issues from year to year, you may be well advised to look for an issue she covered two or three years ago, but not last year.)
The most important thing is that the chart will help you relate your summary of likely issues to the professor's assessment of them as shown in her past exams. Nothing you can do will help you more on the exam.

Writing Your Own Questions

Whether or not old exam questions are available, you should also make up your own test questions. As you review key topics, write down your own exam questions for them. Devising questions should be fairly easy if you've studied actively, summarizing your cases and notes as you've progressed. Be careful not to limit your questions to those you can answer easily; instead, list all the key topics in the course and create mercilessly difficult questions on each of those topics. Write them as though you meant to test and challenge other students. It's sometimes useful to create fact patterns that test several issues or topics at the same time—for example, a pattern that requires you to articulate the difference between battery and assault. And be sure to swap your questions for those your friends create. They may have seen an issue or covered a topic you didn't recognize.

The practice of writing questions raises grades significantly. In one research study, students who made up their own exam questions, incorporating the key points of the course, were able to anticipate 80 percent of the actual exam questions. And, not surprisingly, the grades of these students were 10 percent higher than those of students who didn't make up their own questions. Of course, writing questions takes work and time, so you may be tempted to skip this step. Don't—its proven impact on grades should strengthen your resolve to sit down and write.

Create a "Map" of the Course

By this time, you should have a pretty clear overview of the entire course and be able to see how everything fits together. If you don't feel confident you've achieved this, you may want to try creating a visual map of the entire course. Take a large sheet of paper and create a flowchart, starting at the left, showing every major topic and how it relates to the other topics (these may be crimes, torts, causes of action, etc., depending on the course). For example, to map Civil Procedure, you might follow a case from the initial problems of jurisdiction all the way through to final adjudication. Mapping out the course in this way will give you a good idea what the "forest" looks like, and you'll need to keep this larger picture in mind during your exam. (If the exam is entirely objective rather than essay, you'll have to focus more closely on details, but understanding the "big picture" will still help you in any event; it will show you how the details fit together.)

Cramming

Let's suppose you've ignored all the advice in this book, have skipped a lot of classes, have left gaping holes in your notes, and don't know the cases in your casebook. The exam is looming, and you're in a state of apprehension and panic. Cramming is the worst possible way to study—but you know that. The reality is that, even if you have only a few days left before your exam, you can still pass, but it's more important than ever for you to use your remaining time wisely.

Carefully Schedule Your Studying in the Time You Have Left

Once you realize you're in trouble, you can't afford to lose another minute. If you have only a week before your first exam, spread your studying out over every minute of each day. Above all, don't put your studies off until the day before the exam. Even if you cram for 12 consecutive hours, the material will not be fresh in your mind and you will not do well. Last minute "massed learning" is almost always ineffective. You will be better off studying in five, one-hour sessions over a five-day period than studying in one, ten-hour marathon the day before your exam, even though you'll be studying for only half the number of hours.

If you have only a few days left, the best thing to do is to draw a calendar for each day. First, record all the things you need to do to satisfy your basic needs—meals, sleep, make-up classes. Then divide the rest of the time into 60-minute segments—45 minutes of each segment for study and 15 minutes for a diversionary break. Spend each study segment on a different topic in a different subject. You should be able to fit in at least six study segments each day. That should be enough. In any event, you'll be making the best use of the time you have left.

What to Study

If you must cram, don't reread as many cases as you possibly can or review your outline again and again. Instead, take a more active role in your studies. This is even more important for a "crammer" than it is for people who have studied all semester. Passive reading and rereading will cause your mind to wander. When you have to read a lot of material over a short time, you're likely to get even less out of your reading than you normally would. (To prove this to yourself, try quickly reading three consecutive pages of an outline or a case. Now put them aside. Try to remember what you read. In all likelihood, you'll remember very little.) If you have little time, reading a lot of source material will be of very little help. You should instead spend your time on active study methods, such as writing and answering questions and reviewing old exams.

If you are forced to cram for an exam, old exams and commercial study aids may be your best hope. If you use flashcards, begin by checking your course syllabus and remove any cards from the deck that cover subjects not included in the syllabus. Then, quiz yourself. Follow the advice on mnemonics given in study aids and memorize every mnemonic you come across.

If you have more time, and the test is open-book, you can use canned commercial briefs to study condensed versions of the cases your professor covered. Or read a commercial outline.

Once you've done your substantive review, read Chapter 8, Test-Taking, and review your professor's old exams. *Don't* look over these old exams before you finish your substantive work. They'll only increase your sense of panic, and that's counterproductive. If you're forced to cram, you won't get the best grades on your exams; but, if you use your time wisely and take an active role in your studies, you can at least earn a decent grade. In any event, make it the best grade you can under all the circumstances.

Studying for Objective (Rather than Subjective) Exams

If your exam will be either a multiple-choice or a true/false exam, you should study somewhat differently than you would for an essay exam. As a general rule, objective tests emphasize details, whereas essay questions require an understanding and analysis of overall principles and, sometimes, of several intertwined principles. With essay tests, it's crucial to see the "big picture" of a subject, whereas, for objective exams, you need to lean more heavily on memory and concentrate on details. Objective exams require memorization because they test instant recognition and ask the student to make choices rapidly among several alternatives, whereas essay exams test your ability to absorb and utilize facts, relate rules to facts, and analyze and apply the correct legal principles to a given problem.

Memorization Techniques

The process of memorization—reducing facts and rules to memory—has a bad name in most law schools. Some law professors even claim that you don't need to memorize material for law school exams. The whole process is disparaged in this way because it doesn't appear to require the intellectual abilities professors prize. Remember, though, that you must *remember*, understand, and apply the basic principles recognized by the law in order to score well on exams. If you can't remember the law, you can't apply it, so it is essential to remember the basic principles of each subject.

It is true that, if you have simply memorized the rules of law but don't really understand them and can't apply them, you'll be no better off than if you hadn't memorized them at all. To memorize without understanding is like learning a song in another language—if you don't understand the language, you may be able to repeat the words, but you'll have absolutely no idea what you're saying. Memory is important but it is not enough; you must also understand what you memorize.

Keys to Effective Memorization

To memorize something, you must perform three separate functions: 1) You must record the material in some part of your brain, 2) you must learn to retain it over an indefinite period, and 3) you must be able to retrieve it when you need to use it. If any of these functions fails, you haven't really completed the required process.

The following is a list of what you must to do effectively memorize information.

Actively Self-Test

Memorizing requires that you take an active role in the process. For some people, the entire process is accomplished in one overview of the material. But most people can't simply read something passively and expect to remember it. Instead, they have to take several active steps before the material is firmly lodged in memory.

As you begin your final countdown to exams, test your memory constantly. Force yourself to recite your basic conclusions aloud and to reduce them to notes and questions. Make your mind work—hard. You know the process. You've used it ever since elementary school when you had to learn the words to the "Star Spangled Banner" or multiplication tables or the capital of each state.

Everyone knows the process by which he reduces something to memory. And it differs from person to person. Just make sure that you're utilizing all your own best techniques.

"Chunk" the Material

Organizing material into logical groups makes it easier to remember. If you're not sure what groupings are relevant or helpful, look at the table of contents of a good commercial outline. The author has done the work for you.

Make the Material Meaningful

Books are full of stories of people who could reduce a dictionary to memory without understanding a single word. In law school, the critical function is to understand the meaning behind the words. We can speak the words "Separation of Church and State" without understanding that we are talking about a difficult concept essential to American Constitutional Law. Or we can speak them and at the same time conjure up many different fact patterns, concepts, and issues that test our memory and our understanding of the concept. If you understand how one issue relates to other issues you've already covered (e.g., how the concept of separation relates to religious freedom in general), you'll remember it better. Whenever you can, make connections between one point and another.

Visualize the Material

Try to create a vivid image or picture in your mind of the material you're trying to memorize. If you do, you'll be coding the material in two ways: as written matter that you have read and digested, and again as a mental image engraved firmly in your mind. In this way, you'll be twice as likely to remember it.

Don't Distort the Material

Be careful to record and remember things as they are, not as you think they ought to be. The latter can be tempting when many rules are counterintuitive, or when concepts have misleading titles (e.g., the "Best Evidence Rule" doesn't mean what its name suggests).

Be Mentally Alert (and Concentrate Hard) When You're Memorizing

Research suggests that studying material before you go to sleep increases retention. Sleep seems to solidify the memory by blocking out distractions. (Note, though, that trying to memorize difficult material when you're tired is a waste of time.)

Avoid trying to memorize material as soon as you wake up. The same research indicates that students remember less if they try to study immediately after sleep.

Have Confidence in Your Ability to Memorize

If you're confident of your own ability to memorize, your confidence will stimulate your thought processes and help you remember material. When you study, make sure to think pleasant thoughts and smile periodically. It sounds silly, but you may be surprised at the difference this can make.

You may be a slow learner and therefore conclude you can't memorize easily. But the speed at which you learn says nothing about how long you will remember the material. A bright student may take less time to learn the material, but the student who's not as bright and requires more time to learn the material may retain it better and do just as well on the exam.

Try to be confident about your ability to memorize. If you do, you'll relax. Success in law school depends most on doing every day the things that induce calm and confidence. If you go to class regularly, listen carefully, take good notes, create a thoughtful outline, read your cases and brief them, consult study aids regularly, create your questions and answers, and review the professor's old exams, memory will follow. If there are gaps, you'll recognize them when you go through a study guide and you'll be able to correct them.

Put Other Problems Aside

Anxiety interferes with memory. If you let yourself think about other problems, you won't be able to concentrate on the material you're trying to memorize, and you won't remember if you don't concentrate. This doesn't mean you have to take care of all your other problems before you can begin to memorize; it just means you have to put them aside for the moment. One method that may help you do this is to make a list of everything that's bothering you and then write down how you intend to deal with each item. At the same time, promise yourself to take the steps you've written as soon as you finish your studies. The very act of putting problems and solutions down on paper and then putting the paper aside should help you to put them out of your thoughts for a short time as well.

Watch What You Eat and Drink Before Studying

Make sure you eat before you study. Hunger pangs will distract you from your studies. Also, consider taking vitamins. The vitamins B, C, lecithin, and choline, as well as the amino acid tyrosine, are believed to aid memory.

Don't drink alcohol before—or during—your study sessions. Liquor will shorten your attention span, minimize retention, and make you sleepy. Avoid drugs at all times.

Over-Learning

Don't stop memorizing the first time you think you have the material down pat. In order to engrave the material in your memory indelibly, you must "overlearn" it. Of course, you can take this too far. You'll obtain the maximum benefit for the minimum amount of effort and time if you go over the material one-and-a-half to two times more than the number of times it took you to learn it in the first place. For example, if you are trying to memorize information on a flashcard, and it takes you two tries to recite the answer to the card correctly, review the card once or twice more (a total of three or four times altogether).

Memory Systems: Mnemonics

You've undoubtedly seen ads for courses and books that promise to teach you how to remember everything and claim that you'll never again forget a name, face, or phone number. These ads promise to teach you mysterious, ancient secrets for increasing memory.
In actuality, there's nothing mysterious about the memory process. This section will give you the basics on memory systems; memory systems simply take functions you already use in remembering things (perhaps without even knowing you're using them) and elaborate on them in a special way.

When to Use Mnemonics

If you don't have trouble remembering things, you don't need to use a special memory system. And if you already have a solid grasp of some material, don't waste your time trying to incorporate that material into a new memory system. Rely on your own devices!

What Is a Mnemonic?

The dictionary defines a mnemonic as anything assisting or aiding in memory. This book uses it more precisely to mean a short formula in letters or words that is memorized verbatim and is then recalled when needed to remind you of a larger group of words or phrases constituting a concept, rule, or principle.

Overcoming Your Resistance to Using Mnemonics

Your professors may not be the only ones who believe you shouldn't need mnemonics; perhaps you do, too. You may think that mnemonics are crutches or tricks, or that mnemonics actually give you more to remember and so create more work for you, rather than less.

If the idea of using mnemonics troubles you, it may help to keep in mind what mnemonics are useful for, and what they're not useful for. Mnemonics are not the best way of

❶ remembering material word for word,

❷ remembering abstract concepts, or

❸ performing tasks such as reasoning, analysis, and problem-solving.

Mnemonics are useful only for learning, memorizing, and instant recall.

In your study of law, you'll find mnemonics useful for:

❶ remembering elements and words, and

❷ remembering the major topics.

These two functions, although very simple, are so important to your performance that they justify your use of mnemonics. What mnemonics do is make recall easier and reduce interference with your memory.

The use of mnemonics is also justified when you consider the possible alternatives: thoughtless repetition or simple forgetfulness. (As Maurice Chevalier observed about old age, "It's not so bad when you consider the alternative.") Using mnemonics to remember a connected group of things is infinitely preferable to the alternatives of repeating lists in your mind over and over or forgetting them entirely. Your professor may condemn the use of memory aids, but if you don't remember such facts as the elements of a cause of action, or if you miss issues entirely on your exam, you'll lose points—a very unattractive alternative.

You should note that mnemonics give you "more to memorize" only in the strictest sense: They do require you to memorize a system or code on top of the information you have to memorize anyway. However, mnemonics also make recall easier and more effective. If memorizing a little more material (the mnemonics) makes it easier for you to remember the underlying data you need, then your "memory load" will actually be lightened.

Mnemonics are crutches (or tricks), but so what? On your exam, you'll either remember all the elements of every cause of action, or you won't. You don't get any extra points for using one memory device over another. You should be in favor of any device that helps you perform better, makes your study time more efficient, and allows you to concentrate on analysis and issue-spotting skills instead of worrying about remembering lists of elements.

Types of Mnemonics

"First-Letter" Mnemonics

You're probably most familiar with these types of mnemonics: anagrams, acronyms, and acrostics. For instance, you may be familiar with the acronym for the Great Lakes: HOMES. If you memorize that word, you will find it easier to remember the full names of all five Great Lakes: Huron, Ontario, Michigan, Erie, and Superior. First-letter mnemonics of this sort are a type of "assisted recall." They make lists of words easier to memorize by "chunking" the information, by providing a cue to help you retrieve information from your memory, and by telling you how many items you must remember. "First-letter" mnemonics significantly improve your memory for certain groups of related facts.

In law school, using first-letter mnemonics will help you remember lists of elements, components, and the like. Even more important, first-letter mnemonics can help you remember a list of the major topics in each course, which you can use as a convenient checklist for issue spotting on closed-book exams. Many commercial study aids include helpful mnemonics. You can also make up your own mnemonics for any group of elements you find difficult to remember, as well as create your own mnemonic for an entire course. Once you've created a mnemonic for a list of elements, you need only relate the mnemonic to the details you're trying to recall. With the "HOMES" mnemonic, for example, you could use a mental picture to relate the word "homes" to the Great Lakes; you could visualize all the great cities and the millions of homes clustered around the Great Lakes. Once you've established this relationship, "HOMES" will come to mind whenever you see "Great Lakes," and "HOMES" will remind you of the names of the five lakes.

Acrostics

An acrostic is a device that's closely related to an acronym. To use an acrostic to remember a list, you create a special sentence, using words that will stimulate recall: The first letter of each word in the sentence is also the first letter of a word in the list. (It doesn't matter if the sentence is ridiculous; sometimes a ridiculous sentence is even easier to remember.) For example, the sentence "Every Good Boy Does Fine" is an acrostic that tells you the letter of every note on the lines of the treble clef in music, in ascending order: **E-G-B-D-F**. It will be helpful if you make up acrostics of your own to help you remember lists you have to memorize for your exams (such as the elements of a tort).

Practicing Mnemonics and Acrostics

If you have difficulty memorizing mnemonics (or anything else, for that matter), try using the "10-1-10-1" approach, a method using daily intervals that is based on findings about how memory functions. First, read the mnemonic (or definition or other item) that you want to memorize. Then, put it aside and immediately try to write it down. Repeat this process until you've written it perfectly. Stop writing. Wait ten minutes, and try to write it again. Check your result and fill in any gaps, then stop again. Wait one hour, and write it down again. Wait ten hours, and write it again. Wait one day, and write it again. These intervals—ten minutes, one hour, ten hours, and one day—are intervals at which memory is believed to break down, so, if you study in those intervals, you should forestall forgetting and eventually engrave the mnemonic in your memory.

After you memorize a mnemonic, you must reinforce your memory periodically until you take your exam. Write down the mnemonic as frequently as you find necessary in order to cement it into your memory. You may choose to write it every day or two to enable you to remember every element flawlessly.

Using Visual Imagery

Another powerful memory tool for law school exams is visual imagery: creating a mental picture for a word or concept. For some people, images are more memorable than words, and words that conjure up images help to "dual-code" (imprinting the material in both your verbal and your visual memory). A person is more likely to remember words that have been paired with visual images.

Create your own visual associations for any concepts you find difficult to remember. To make your images even more memorable, be as creative as you can. Think of word pictures that are vivid or even bizarre. For instance, to help remember that contracts in consideration of marriage must be in writing (to satisfy the Statute of Frauds), you might picture a giant fountain pen in a wedding dress, gliding across the signature line of a contract as big as a football field. The more unusual the picture, the easier it will be to remember. Be careful not to create too many images, though. It's easy to become enamored of your creations, but they take time to create and sometimes the time is better spent in other study activities, such as exam-question review.

Other Memory Systems: Peg, Link, and Loci

The Peg System

A peg system uses concrete words (called "peg" words) to stand for numbers with which they rhyme. Choose words that rhyme with the numbers one through ten: one might equal sun; two, shoe; three, tree; and so forth. (Instead of numbers, you could use the alphabet.) You then create a mental picture by linking each word on your list with a creative, unforgettable visual image. The last step is to link the image with the legal rule or principle you want to recall.

A Link System

With a "link" system, you memorize a series of items by first creating a bizarre mental image for each item, and then creating a story that links the items together.

The Loci System

The loci memory system is a method of association by organization, rather than association by exaggerated or bizarre imagery (which the peg and link systems use). To use a loci system, you label parts of a building (such as your house). You then put a stimulus for each topic in a separate room. When you want to remember the items on a list, you mentally "walk through" your locations, in order, and "see" or recall what's there and then associate it with the underlying principle.

Rhymes and Jingles

You probably already use these, often without realizing it. One common rhyme used as a memory aid teaches the number of days in a month: "Thirty days hath September, April, June, and November. . . ." The music found in commercial ads constitutes memory-aid jingles; you probably know several by heart (which testifies to their power as memory enhancers). The most effective jingles use a simple rhythm and a strong beat. If you're industrious enough to create your own jingles or rhymes, practice reciting or singing them aloud. This will help you remember them: When your ears hear a jingle, the melody and the rhythm will help your brain recall the words.

Rote Memorization

This is mentioned last because it's really not part of a memory system. It's also the least time-effective system for remembering. With rote memorization, you simply go over and over something until it's fixed in your memory. If you choose to memorize using this method, you'll do best by breaking up the material into logical parts, repeating each part several times, and reciting it aloud. When you think you "have it," repeat it again three or four times. Then go on to something else, then come back after an hour or so and repeat it again several times.

This method, which works better than others for some of us, requires one thing—constant and frequent repetition of the ingredients—preferably aloud, and, even better, to someone who will listen.

CHAPTER 8
Test-Taking

In this chapter, you'll reap the reward for all your hard work: You'll learn how to apply all your knowledge to achieve the highest possible grades on your exams.

This chapter doesn't deal with learning the law. Instead, it addresses the skills of "examsmanship." Superior examsmanship means the ability to communicate your knowledge accurately and effectively. If you have a great deal of knowledge but lack examsmanship, you may receive a B or a C on your exam when you should have earned an A. If you develop solid exam-taking skills, you'll earn a higher grade than a classmate who has the same level of knowledge but lacks the exam skills.

First, assume that you've learned everything taught in the previous pages. You've memorized all the definitions, rules, rationales, and policies; you've mastered a course mnemonic, as well as all the other mnemonics you've created or adopted; and you can recognize the issues that appear in fact patterns and can apply the correct rules and definitions to them. You need this knowledge to get your best grade. An "A" performance on a law exam is a synthesis of your knowledge and examsmanship. You need both to reach the "A" level; neither works without the other.

This chapter deals with typical law school exam material, including sample questions and answers. To illustrate, read the sample question and answer below:

Your Exam in Criminal Law: A Sample Question

Andy, a college senior, buys a realistic-looking toy gun that shoots red dye. It's used in a game called "Killer," the object of which is to "shoot" the other players and say, "Bang, you're dead," before they shoot you.

Andy goes to a local public park one morning with his friend, Brad, to play "Killer." Both are armed with the toy guns. Andy hides behind a row of tall hedges, waiting for Brad. He hears Brad coming and jumps out. In fact, it's not Brad at all, but Carl, an off-duty cop, and his wife, Ellen. Before Andy realizes this, he has aimed the gun at Carl. He yells, "Bang, you're dead," and fires, hitting Carl with dye. Ellen screams. Carl, believing that the gun is real and that he's been shot, whips out his pistol, which he's licensed to carry. He fires at Andy, hitting him in the chest. Andy falls to the ground, unconscious. Carl asks Ellen to call an ambulance. While Ellen runs to call, Carl stays and administers first aid to Andy. Daniel, a stranger to all, is jogging by and sees the toy gun lying next to Andy's hand. Believing it's a real gun, Daniel grabs it and runs off. Carl fails to notice Daniel until he's out of sight. Andy subsequently recovers from his injuries.

Daniel runs to the local bank, carrying the gun, and approaches the counter. He waves the gun at the bank patrons and tellers, shouting, "Customers, hit the floor! Tellers, give me all your money! Do as I say or you're all dead!" The tellers freeze, and most of the customers quickly hit the floor. Customer Farley, an off-duty bank guard, slowly reaches for his gun, which is licensed. Daniel aims the toy gun at Farley and tells him, "Don't even think about it, wise guy. Throw your gun down and kick it over to me, real gentle-like." Farley kicks over his gun, but, when Daniel puts his foot on it to stop it, it accidentally goes off, killing customer Gordon. Daniel picks the gun up. Farley moves toward Daniel. Daniel fires the toy gun at him, covering him with dye. Both Farley and Daniel are momentarily stunned. Then Daniel, realizing what has happened, shoots and kills Farley with Farley's gun. Police officer Malloy, walking by on his way to a doughnut shop, sees Daniel shoot Farley and fires his gun at Daniel. He misses Daniel but hits teller Iris, killing her. In the melee, Daniel flees the bank without getting any money and gets away.

Discuss the criminal liability of Andy, Carl, and Daniel.

Sample Answer

Andy's Liability for Shooting Carl with Dye

Andy (A) is guilty of both assault and battery on Carl (C). Criminal assault is either an intentional attempt to commit a battery or the intentional creation of fear of imminent bodily harm in the mind of the victim. Thus, there are two elements to consider: 1) A's intent and 2) C's perception. A's act of raising the gun at C would satisfy the intent element because the act of pointing the gun at C was intentional. C's belief that the gun was real would create the fear in his mind that A would shoot him. Since both elements are satisfied, A will be guilty of assault on C.

A will also be guilty of battery on C. Criminal battery is an unlawful application of force to the person of another, resulting in either bodily injury or an offensive touching. Here, the dye touched C; even if the touching didn't hurt C, it would be considered an offensive touching. Thus, A is guilty of battery on C.

Andy's Liability to Ellen

A may also be guilty of assault on Ellen (E). The issues as to E would be: 1) whether A intended to create a fear in her of imminent bodily harm to her when he pointed the the gun at her husband, although not at her, and 2) whether pointing the gun did actually create this fear in her mind. Both of these issues turn on E's reasonable perception based upon her proximity to C. A's aiming the gun in E's general direction would signal A's intent; whether she was reasonably in fear of imminent bodily harm to herself would depend on her proximity to C. The fact that she screamed, and that it's reasonably inferable from the facts that she must have been standing next to C when the "shooting" occurred, would make it likely that she did reasonably fear imminent bodily harm to herself, as well as that A, by raising a gun in her direction, intended this harm. Thus, A will probably be found liable for assault on her. If, however, E was not sufficiently close to C to create a reasonable fear for her safety and if she screamed only because C was being shot, the requirement of the fear of injury to herself would be missing and a court would not hold A liable for assault on E.

Carl's Liability for Shooting Andy

C will probably be charged with attempted murder but should escape conviction on grounds of self-defense. Common-law murder is an unlawful killing with malice aforethought. Attempt requires the intent to commit murder and an overt act (beyond mere preparation) done in furtherance of that intent. C actually shot A, going well beyond mere preparation, so that the element of "attempt" exists. "Unlawful" means that the killing must be neither justifiable nor excusable. Here, the unlawful element is missing because the attempt was justifiable: C shot A in what he reasonably thought was self-defense. Self-defense is a valid defense when an intended victim uses the force that seems reasonably necessary to protect himself from an attacker's use of unlawful force on him. The victim's belief in the threat of harm must be reasonable, and the force used by him must be reasonable. C believed the gun was real, and since the gun looked real, a court would probably find his belief of imminent harm reasonable. This, coupled with the fact that C thought A had shot him, would make the use of force reasonable. Further, the amount of force used was reasonable. Deadly force is only merited when one is threatened with great bodily harm or death. Here, since C thought he was about to be killed, his use of deadly force in response was merited.

If C's belief that the gun was real was found unreasonable, in some states he would be liable for manslaughter, but not murder, under the imperfect self-defense doctrine. Under this doctrine, murder is reduced to manslaughter where the belief that deadly force is justified is honest, but unreasonable. In states where this doctrine isn't recognized, if C's belief that the gun was real was not found reasonable, he would be guilty of attempted murder, since the attempted killing was unlawful, and he had malice, manifested by his intent to kill A or to cause him great bodily injury, as indicated by his shooting A in the chest.

Daniel's Liability

1. For Taking the Gun

Daniel (D) would be guilty of larceny for taking the toy gun. A larceny is a trespassory taking and carrying away of personal property of another with intent to steal it. D's taking the gun and running away with it would satisfy the elements of larceny. However, he would not be guilty of robbery. Robbery is a larceny from the person or presence of the owner, accomplished with force or fear. D did not use force to take the gun. Further, A was unconscious and C didn't see D, so no victim was put in fear.

D is also not guilty of assault on either A or C. Since A was unconscious and C didn't see D, there was no apprehension of imminent bodily harm, an essential element of assault.

2. For Trying to Rob the Bank

D would be guilty of attempted robbery as to the bank. D's shouts establish his intent to rob the bank; those statements, coupled with the use of the gun and its effect on the tellers and customers, satisfy the "force or fear" element of robbery. Finally, his actions would satisfy the element of "attempt" because they went "beyond mere preparation." Also, D would not have a valid defense of abandonment because abandonment must be motivated by a voluntary relinquishment of the criminal intent. Here, D fled the bank because of the shootings, not because he no longer intended to rob the bank. Furthermore, his departure was not voluntary; D fled only because things weren't going his way and he knew he was in trouble. Thus, he has no abandonment defense.

3. For Aiming the Gun at the Tellers, Patrons, and Farley

D would be guilty of assault. By waving the gun at everyone in the bank, D created in them the fear of imminent offensive contact; this, coupled with his intent to instill fear, would create an assault.

4. For Holding the Tellers and Patrons at Bay with the Gun

D would be guilty of unlawful imprisonment as to the tellers, the patrons, and Farley (F). Unlawful imprisonment is the intentional confinement or physical restraint of a person, amounting to a significant interference with her freedom of movement, without that person's consent. In the facts as given, D confined both tellers and patrons in the bank by threatening them with a gun.

5. For Killing Gordon

D would be guilty of felony murder as a result of Gordon (G)'s death. A person is guilty of felony murder if a homicide occurs during the commission by him of a dangerous felony or an attempt to commit that felony, even if there's no intent to kill or to cause great bodily harm. Attempted robbery with the use of a gun is a dangerous felony because it carries with it the natural and probable consequence of bodily harm. While D didn't intend to kill G, this doesn't matter, because felony murder doesn't require that the killing itself be intentional; it's sufficient if the killing is the proximate consequence of the other felony. Here, D took F's gun as part of the robbery, so the proximate cause element is satisfied.

6. For Killing Farley

D would be guilty of battery (see above) and attempted murder for shooting the dye in the toy gun at F and guilty of murder for killing him with the real gun.

Shooting F with the dye would be attempted murder because D intended to kill F and had no excuse or justification for doing so. Also, he went beyond mere preparation; he did everything he thought he needed to do to commit the crime of murder. It doesn't matter that he couldn't, in fact, kill F with the toy gun. The policy behind attempted crimes is to punish those who manifest their willingness to commit crimes, not just to thwart crime, and since D manifested his intent to harm F here, he would be guilty of attempt. Even if D were not liable for attempt, he would be liable for battery, on the same basis that A was liable for battery on C: shooting the dye would be considered unlawful force, and the dye on F would be considered an offensive touching.

D would be guilty of murder for killing F with F's gun since he had no justification or excuse for shooting F, and he satisfies the "malice" requirement since he intended, if not to kill Farley, then at least to inflict serious bodily injury on him.

7. For Malloy's Killing of Iris

There is a split of authority on whether a defendant who commits a dangerous felony can be charged with felony murder when he himself does not commit the killing. In some jurisdictions, D would be guilty under the felony murder rule; in others, he would not be because he did not shoot Iris (I).

Under the felony murder rule, one is liable for homicides committed during and as a result of a dangerous felony (or an attempted dangerous felony). In some jurisdictions, it's not material that the killing was done by someone other than the perpetrator, as long as the homicide results from the commission of the felony. Here, Malloy (M)'s killing of I was the direct result of D's trying to rob the bank: M was trying to thwart the robbery by attempting to shoot the perpetrator (D). As a result, D would be liable in these jurisdictions. The issue is one of causation: but for the dangerous felony committed by D, M would not have used his gun to shoot at D, and I would not have been shot.

In other jurisdictions, the issue would be M's justification in shooting I. Because M was trying to stop a dangerous felony, the consequential death of I would be deemed the consequence of a justifiable act. In those jurisdictions, D would not be liable for I's death.

Preliminary Observations About the Model Answer

Note that the above answer is a "model" answer, not a "perfect" answer. Keep that distinction in mind: You can't write a "perfect" answer; no one can. Your answer won't be compared to one that some perfect, mythical law student would write; rather, your answer will be graded by comparison with your classmates' answers. (Keep that fact in mind when looking at sample answers provided by your professor or a commercial outline.)

A law school exam is like a game: Your team doesn't have to get a set number of points to win, it just has to get more points than the other team. Thus, to get an A on your exam, you only have to get more points than most of your classmates. You won't be required to spot all the elements of every issue, or to discuss every possible applicable theory; also, you won't have to reach all the "right" conclusions. In fact, you'd be surprised to learn how different most "A" answers to the same question can be. All "A" answers will spot the basic issues and demonstrate a similar level of analysis; apart from that, they'll differ widely.

How Professors Create Exams

You may believe that exam questions come from some mysterious source, or that your professor has a rare and hard-earned talent for creating exam questions. In most cases, that's not true. Your professor probably has no particular training in creating exams: she went to law school, clerked or practiced law for awhile, and then became a teacher. Therefore, her exams are likely to resemble the kind of exams she took in law school, or the exams of other faculty members to whom she has turned for advice.

Most professors create exams by first listing the concepts they wish to test, and then devising questions (in the form of hypothetical fact patterns) to test those concepts. In the sample question, the professor wanted to test the crime of homicide. While larceny, robbery, and other crimes are included in the question, they're actually minor points in this question; similar facts testing those points more extensively might appear in other questions. In order to test you fairly and thoroughly, your professor will probably create questions that address every major concept she covered in class. If she were to create a criminal law exam that focused exclusively on one area (such as conspiracy), the exam wouldn't be an accurate indicator of how well you'd learned the course material overall: you might be well prepared on every other aspect of criminal law, but simply weak on conspiracy. In order for an exam to reflect what it should (assuming that your professor is fair), the exam will test all the major areas in the course, not just a few.

In addition, your professor may create questions aimed at various levels of skill and knowledge. She may ask a question that tests only whether a student can spot issues; that question may be pitched at the lowest level of proficiency and knowledge. She may expect only the totally incompetent to fail it. Law school exams can be designed to test a variety of skills, including legal analysis and problem solving. This is the skill level at which most exam questions are "pitched." You may also face questions that require you to synthesize conflicting rules and create a new rule, or to make predictions about how a court might resolve a thorny theoretical problem. These questions require that you understand the fundamentals of the law and know how to apply them, not simply that you recall black-letter definitions. Questions at this higher level force you to think about the law, and especially about the rationales/policies behind the rules, and then apply them to an unresolved situation. Questions of this type are difficult to grade under uniform standards, so they don't appear often on exams, but you must be prepared to deal with them.

How Professors Grade Exams

There are two basic ways in which professors grade exams. Understanding these methods will help you write answers that will get you the most points.

Using a Key

Some professors grade exams by using an answer "key." They allocate a range of fixed points for measures such as issue spotting, rule statements, discussions, and conclusions. Generally, they'll give more weight to issues that they concentrated on, and they'll allot fewer points to issues they obviously considered less important. (Thus, it's crucial you learn to recognize what your professor considers important). Most professors grade exams in this way because it's probably the only method that ensures

consistency in grading. To give you an idea what an answer key
looks like, here's one constructed for the model answer:

Total points	Topic
	A's liability for shooting C
7	Assault on C (seeing issue)
2	Definition
4	Discussion (A's perspective and C's perspective)
1	Conclusion
8	Battery (seeing issue)
2	Definition
3	Discussion
2	Conclusion
5	Assault on E (seeing issue)
3	Discussion (reasonability of fear)
2	Conclusion
	C's liability for shooting A
10	Attempted murder (seeing issue)
3	Definition/attempt
3	Definition/murder/other homicides
3	Definition/self-defense
8	Discussion (reasonable belief, imperfect self-defense)
3	Conclusion
	D's liability
	For taking gun:
8	Larceny (seeing issue)
2	Definition
3	Discussion
2	Conclusion
3	Robbery (seeing issue)
1	Definition
2	Discussion (no force or fear)
1	Conclusion
2	Assault (seeing issue)
1	Discussion
	In trying to rob bank:
6	Attempted robbery (seeing issue)
2	Definition

Total points	Topic
4	Discussion (abandonment defense)
1	Conclusion
5	Assault (seeing issue)
2	Definition
4	Discussion
1	Conclusion
5	Unlawful imprisonment (seeing issue)
2	Definition
3	Discussion
1	Conclusion

For killing G

8	Felony murder (seeing issue)
2	Definition
2	Discussion (was crime sufficient)
3	Discussion (proximity to crime)
2	Discussion (no intent required)
2	Conclusion

For killing F

4	Attempted murder (seeing issue)
2	Definition
4	Discussion (toy gun make difference?)
1	Conclusion
8	Murder (seeing issue)
2	Definition
4	Discussion
1	Conclusion

For Malloy's killing of Iris

8	Felony murder (seeing issue)
2	Definition
7	Discussion (liability for justifiable killings)
2	Conclusion
10	Overall quality points (other issues)

Take note of four important features about this answer key:

✔ Spotting the Big Issues

Professors give the greatest number of points for spotting the big issues and for your discussion of these issues. The prize goes to those students who concentrate on the big issues, not to those who try to make points on minor "glimmer" issues.

✔ The Points Don't Add Up to 100

Professors could make the points add up to an even hundred, but there's no particular reason to do this. So long as each student is judged under the same key, the professor will be able to measure the relative value of each student's performance.

✔ There Are Ten Unassigned "Quality Points" at the End

A professor may want to include overall "quality" points to reward students for spotting issues the professor didn't see, or for making a particularly compelling argument. (Note, however, that it takes a lot of ingenuity to impress a professor enough to assign points to these "extras," so don't spend a lot of time trying to "outsmart" or impress your professor).

✔ Items in Parentheses

The items in parentheses after many of the "discussion" sections indicate the areas the professor would expect you to cover in your answer.

Note: Of course, one professor's "key" will not be the same as another's, even in the same subject. When you take the exam, you don't need to concern yourself with your professor's possible key. Just remember that it will be based essentially on your recognition and discussion of issues, and do the best you can.

The "Holistic" Method of Grading

A professor who grades holistically will read each student's answer and compare it with a loosely defined standard arrived at by his overall impression of the quality of all the answers submitted for that exam. This method emphasizes the relative quality of each exam paper. In holistic grading, no points are assigned for any particular skill; rather, the professor judges the quality of each exam as a whole when compared in a general and loose way to all others.

Relatively few professors use this method. Those who do generally "pre-read" a random selection of exam answers to get a feel for the range and relative quality of responses. This will enable them to see whether a question was confusing; whether some of the issues were so unclear that even the best students were unable to spot them; and, in general, what relative levels of response to expect from the answers. The answers are then mixed back into the pile.

At this point, the professor reads all the students' answers, separating them into different piles according to quality. (That is, he will make a pile containing what he believes to be the "better" answers, one containing the "average" answers, and one containing the "poorer" answers.) Then, the professor reviews the answers in each pile, ranking the answers in that pile according to their quality. Having thus arranged all the answers in order, from strongest to weakest, the professor then assigns the appropriate grade to each.

Idiosyncratic Grading Methods

Even so, not all professors use either the "key" method or the "holistic" method. Some professors simply read one exam answer after another, getting an overall impression of each as they go and assigning a grade that is only approximately related to the grade that answer might have received under a more organized approach.

Whatever the grading system, you have to recognize three important facts. Bear these in mind as you read on.

You Can't Afford to Overlook the Issues Raised by the Question

The test taker's single most important task on any law school exam question is to recognize the issues. If you look at the above exam key, you will see that it has assigned more than 42 percent of all the points to recognition of the issues. Whether or not your professor uses the key method, she will do the same thing by whatever grading method. Since the skills for spotting issues get sharper and sharper with practice, it is incredibly important to practice with old exams.

After spotting the issues, you have to define and discuss them with such precision that your professor knows that you understand them. This requires clarity of thought and expression. These skills can also be improved with practice, and there are several commercial study aids that are designed to develop exam-taking skills. Look at what is available at your law school bookstore or in your school's academic support program office.

Your Performance Is Relative

If you write an exam that is relatively good when everyone else submits a terrible one, you'll still get the top grade. (Although you may not get an A; the professor may decide that the whole class needs to be shaken up.) Conversely, if you write a good answer but everyone else writes an excellent one, your grade will be relatively low, even though your performance in both cases is exactly the same. All you can expect of yourself is to work as hard as you can to develop the necessary skills and to communicate what you know in the most effective manner you can.

The Exam's Level of Difficulty Won't Matter

Because you're graded relative to your classmates, it doesn't really matter how difficult the exam is. If a professor writes a difficult question, the average grade earned by students in the class will be lower, but there will still be students who earn more points than the average, as well as students who earn fewer. Interestingly, professors who are skilled at testing tend to make their exams relatively easier, rather than harder. If they create exams in which only 5 percent of the students can spot a "hidden" issue, the results are worthless. A good exam will evaluate students across the range of ability and knowledge throughout the class, not just those who happen to be in sync with the professor's "tricks."

Pre-Exam Advice
The Night Before the Exam

The secret to good test-taking is to be relaxed at exam time. If you've kept up with your work during the semester and followed most of this book's advice, you have the exam nailed. Let others hyperventilate; you're going to shine. You're mentally prepared. You've studied, outlined, and memorized everything you need to know. You can tell yourself—and truly believe—that you're going to perform to the best of your ability.

The night before your exam, limit your review time to two or three hours. Break down that time as you did your other study sessions; ideally, you should study for no more than 45 minutes at a time, with 15-minute breaks in between. By exam time, you should be doing only "big picture" review, making sure that you've memorized your outline and any mnemonics you have found useful.

Stop studying at least one hour (preferably two) before you plan to go to bed. If you don't, you may have difficulty falling asleep. During that final waking hour or two, do something unrelated to studying. The further removed your pre-sleep activity is from studying, the less likely it is that the activity will "interfere" with your memory. If you watch TV, watch something light.

You should plan on getting a normal night's sleep. Some people suggest getting a lot of sleep before an exam, but too much sleep can make you just as tired and ineffective as too little sleep. You've taken a lot of crucial exams by this time in your life as a student. At this point, you probably know what works best for you.

On the day of the exam, try not to think about the exam or discuss it with your fellow students. It's too late for you to learn anything that will have any impact on your grade, so the only consequence of this type of discussion at this point is to make you feel panicky ("My God, he knows something I don't know!"). If you're well-prepared, you have nothing to gain by talking with other students before the exam.

Instead, use the time before the exam to eat a light meal. This will give you energy but won't make you sleepy. Right before the test, get some exercise. A brisk walk, for instance, will promote circulation and get more oxygen to your brain. (Don't make your pre-exam exercise so strenuous, however, that you feel exhausted or sleepy.)

Take a watch (or a battery-run clock) and a calculator to the exam, along with any other materials you're allowed to take. (If you are typing your exam on a computer, you can use it to keep track of time, but make sure whatever special software your school uses for exams doesn't interfere with the clock.) If they're allowed, don't forget your indexed outline and textbook (e.g., for an open-book exam). You should also bring earplugs if your school doesn't provide them.

During the exam, earplugs will block the noise of students coughing, rustling papers, writing, or perhaps even crying (which you won't be doing because you adequately prepared). Earplugs will enfold you in your own exam-taking world and you can concentrate on spotting the issues rather than your sniffling classmate's cold.

You may be allowed to bring food and beverages into the exam. However, don't be the student who brings a bag of chips—you will be hated. Bring bottled water with a spill-proof cap and perhaps a small piece of candy (already unwrapped) or sliced fruit in case you get an attack of the munchies midway through your three-hour exam. Remember, however, that any time spent in the restroom is time you will not spend writing, so limit your intake of liquids.

Finally, get to the test site early. Find a comfortable seat in a comfortable spot, and, as you did for every class session, get yourself ready mentally. Don't do any last-minute cramming while you're waiting for the exam to begin—you'll only make yourself nervous. If people around you are discussing the test, ignore them. If you brought an iPod, put on the headphones to avoid this "exam chatter." If you brought earplugs, insert them now. If you need something to do, bring along Silly Putty or a stress ball to take care of any last-minute jitters. Keep telling yourself that you can and will succeed, and that this is your one great opportunity to show how well you know the material.

When You Begin the Exam

① **STEP ONE: Write an Outline of the Basics**

As soon as you receive your exam and scratch paper, take a sheet of the scratch paper and write your general topic outline horizontally down one side of the page. Fill in each topic and subtopic. Then write down any mnemonics you have found useful. Next, write down any major rules or definitions you have found hard to use or remember. All this should take no more than two or three minutes, and it's not a waste of time. Taking a few minutes at the beginning to write down these all-important items will leave you free to look for issues and analyze them, rather than hunt through your memory again and again during the exam. Writing down the ingredients you need as soon as you start will dramatically reduce your anxiety and improve your performance.

Once all the basics are down on scrap paper, you're ready to look at the exam.

② **STEP TWO: Read the Instructions—Again**

As obvious as this may seem, many students ignore the instructions on their exams. Don't do this! Individual professors have idiosyncrasies that you must take into account and follow. If your professor wants you to write on every other line, not go over a certain number of words or lines, or give a conclusion for each question at the start of your answer instead of the close, follow the instructions. If you ignore them, you will both incur the professor's ill will and stamp yourself as either an illiterate or a stubborn ass who will not follow instructions.

③ **STEP THREE: Skim the Entire Exam First**

Before you begin to work on any one question, skim over the entire exam *briefly*. For each question, glance first at the "call" of the question: that is, what it's asking you to do. The "call" will appear at the end of the question. In the sample question, for example, the call is: "Discuss the criminal liability of A, C, and D." After identifying the call, go back and read the question at your "normal" rate—that is, the rate at which you'd read a newspaper article. For help later, put one checkmark next to easy questions, two checks next to moderately difficult ones, and three checks next to very difficult ones. This approach has several benefits:

It Helps with Issue Spotting

Your professor is unlikely to test the same issue or rule in two different questions. After you've glanced through the entire test, you'll have a pretty good idea what issues are covered in each question. You won't look for a "hidden" issue in one question that's clearly covered in detail in another one. Keep in mind that your professor is trying to test your knowledge of the class as a whole, so each question will stand for a set of unique issues (e.g., a poisonous factory question might be asking you to discuss abnormally hazardous activities, while a question on the same exam involving swimming with sharks might be asking you to discuss simple negligence, not abnormally hazardous activities again).

You Have Identified the Easy Questions and Can Complete Them First

This helps in two ways. First, it ensures that you'll do a very good job on questions you find easy. Second, it will enable you to get a number of questions out of the way quickly. This will increase your confidence in your ability to get through the rest of the exam. Hitting the easy questions first will also avoid the tendency of some students to "try" the tough questions at the beginning. This tendency results in a lot of lost time and unnecessary "panic." After you've finished the easy questions, you can go on to the moderately difficult ones and then the hardest ones. This approach of moving through the questions in order of their apparent difficulty will be most productive for the average student.

Reading the Whole Exam Helps "Cue" Your Mind for the Issues and Rules

Reading the entire exam through before answering any questions gives your mind a chance to pick up cues in some of the questions that may trigger issues in others. For example, a question on attempted robbery in a criminal law exam may trigger recognition of the elements required for "attempt" in the context of a question involving a homicide.

Warning

Even so, you shouldn't spend too much time evaluating the questions. Take no more than five or so minutes—you'll want to use most of your time outlining and writing your answers.

④ **STEP FOUR: Create a Per-Question Time Schedule**

Now that you've read the entire exam and listed the questions in order of difficulty, it's time to create a time schedule that you'll adhere to strictly. Determine how much time you'll spend on each question by comparing its value to that of the other questions. If you have a three-hour final, consisting of three questions, and you're told that each question is worth one-third of the exam (33 percent of your grade), spend one-third of your time on each question. (Modify this commitment, however, by spending less time on a question you find easy and saving the time for a question that seems more difficult.) At the outset, never spend a minute more than your time schedule permits for any single question. If you save some time as you work through the answers, you can always go back. In a three-hour exam, it is a classic law student mistake to spend, for example, two hours on the first one-hour question, 45 minutes on the second one-hour question, and 15 minutes on the third one-hour question. Even if you write the most complete answer in the class for question one, it won't make up for your poor performance on the next two questions.

Alternatively, your professor may give you time values for each question (e.g., "this is a one-hour question" or "a 45-minute question"). You will have to modify these times slightly to reflect the time you spent writing your outline and mnemonics and skimming the exam (perhaps five minutes); also, you should allow for another five minutes that you may waste somehow during the exam (after all, you're not a machine). In a three-question, three-hour final, with equally weighted questions, you'll have 170 minutes left over for the questions if you apply these calculations. This is approximately 57 minutes per question. (A calculator can come in handy for figuring times; even simple calculations can fluster you when you're under pressure.) Write your target start and end times above each question, *and stick to them.*

⑤ **STEP FIVE: Tackling the First Question You Choose to Answer**

The first question you answer should be the one you found the easiest (the one you marked with a single check) when you skimmed the exam. Before you begin, write down the time you will commit to this question on your scratch paper. For instance, if the exam began at 9:00 and you spent five minutes writing your outline and skimming the exam, you might write down "finish 10:02" on your scratch paper (9:05 plus 57 minutes). This way, you won't have to continually recalculate your completion time, and you'll be more likely to stick to your time schedule.

Your First Reading of the First Question

Read the "call" of the question *carefully*. This will tell you both how to direct and limit your analysis and which viewpoint to take. In the above sample question, your viewpoint will be that of an objective observer—you weren't assigned a specific role to play. However, professors sometimes ask you to play a defined role when you analyze and write. For example, the question may direct you to act as lawyer for one of the defendants, tell you that a judge has asked you to write an appellate opinion dealing with the findings and conclusions of a lower court, or that you're a law clerk who's been assigned to write a memo about a specific issue for a senior partner who's representing one of the parties. In any question, your analysis of the facts and the issues will necessarily depend on the role you're asked to play, so read the call and the instructions with a great deal of care. If you get these wrong, you'll go off on the wrong trail and actually prevent yourself from doing your best. Most of all, you'll confuse and annoy your professor and preclude a fair analysis of your ability.

Also, the call of the question may cut down on the scope of your analysis. In the sample question, you're told that you need only analyze the liability of A, C, and D. You don't have to analyze the criminal liability of any other party because that's not part of the call and, therefore, not part of your instructions. You need to search only for those issues bearing on the legal liability of those three, however enticing some other issues may seem and however much you may want to display your erudition on related points. Note also that the call in the sample question is very broad in scope: "Discuss the criminal liability of. . . ." It could easily have been more narrow or limited. For instance, the call might have asked you to

❶ discuss Carl's liability for shooting Andy,

❷ discuss Daniel's liability for shooting Farley, and

❸ discuss Daniel's liability for Malloy's shooting of Iris.

If so, you'd deal with those three issues and no others. This is a very important point because, on some questions, you'll be very tempted to expand the scope of the question. Since you've studied hard and know a lot about each subject, you will want to discuss every issue you spot. Fight the temptation, or you'll waste valuable time. Worst of all, you'll get no extra points. In Torts, for example, if the call of the question directs you to discuss intentional torts, put negligence out of your mind—writing about any issues you see in the facts relating to negligence won't help you.

In Contracts, you may be told specifically to ignore any promissory estoppel issues. If so, don't even look for them—blot them out of your mind. Remember, you're being tested on how well you can follow instructions and perform an assigned task. Showing that you can perform some other task doesn't prove either—on the contrary, it proves just the reverse. And you won't be allotted a single extra point on the exam. Look at the sample question and at the answer key—if you ignored the instructions and discussed Malloy's liability, you wasted valuable time and accomplished nothing. Malloy's liability doesn't even appear on the answer key—so, absolutely zero points.

Finally, make sure you interpret the call of the question correctly and completely and every issue that it implies or suggests. Remember, you may decide to discard some issues as irrelevant or unimportant, but you've got to be able to see them first.

For instance, in the sample question, you're asked to discuss the criminal liability of Andy, Carl, and Daniel. You must, therefore, discuss not only the crimes for which each is potentially liable, but also any defenses he may have. (Remember, you're being asked for *liability*, and he can't be *liable* if he has a valid defense.)

In the same way, if you're asked for the *liability* of one party in a contract question, you're really being asked to look for and discuss all of the following: Are all the elements of a contract present; is there a valid contract; has any party breached; has our party breached; if so, are any defenses available to our party; and what remedies does our party have? Of all these, the average student is most likely to overlook defenses and remedies; since it's a rare problem that doesn't include either or both, be sure you include them in your analysis.

Your Second Reading of the Question

Once you've read *and understood* the call of the question, go back and read the question again, slowly. Read slowly enough to read every word carefully, but not so slowly that you lose the thread of the question. Try to visualize the fact pattern as a whole. This is useful for two reasons.

First, if the facts bearing on a certain issue are described in different parts of the question, you may miss some of them when you're focusing excessively on each word. In the sample question, for instance, D's potential liability for the hold-up will turn on whether he completed the crime or not—if he did, it would be robbery; if he didn't, it would be attempted robbery. The facts that spell out the answer (i.e., the attempt and the ultimate flight, without money) are in several different places in the question. To see them all, you have to picture all the action taking place in the facts.

Second, understanding the question as a whole will prevent you from missing a point altogether. If you don't get the overall picture, the assumptions you make will be wrong, and your answer will contain serious mistakes.

Understanding the question as a whole requires that you record and retain *all* the material events. In a torts question, these may be the events leading to injury; in a contracts question, they may be all the events bearing on the creation or breach of a contractual duty; in a criminal law question, they may be all the events leading to or surrounding the commission of some act or acts that are defined as criminal. As you read, you must record the material events in the order they occur. It's a good idea to describe each one in the margin and to assign it a sequential number. Write down everything that happens, as well as the name of every party.

Each time a party is mentioned, you have to record all events that relate to that party. Generally, a professor won't include a party in her question without a good reason. For example, if a question refers to the commission of a crime or a tort by two people rather than one you can be fairly certain their liability will diverge at some point and that you have to analyze the facts for each. (In criminal law questions, always consider the possibility of conspiracy.) A professor may sometimes include a party for the sake of humor, or as a red herring. This only means that you have to be ever-vigilant to recognize the presence and relevance of each party.

In the sample question, these are the material events:

❶ Andy has toy gun.
❷ Andy shoots Carl in presence of Ellen.
❸ Carl shoots Andy.
❹ Daniel takes toy gun, believing it's real.

❺ Daniel runs to bank and attempts robbery.
❻ Daniel accidentally fires Farley's gun, killing Gordon.
❼ Daniel fires toy gun and then Farley's gun at Farley, killing Farley.
❽ Police Officer Malloy fires at and misses Daniel, but shoots and kills teller Iris.

That's it—the framework of the entire question and of the answer. On your first reading of the question, don't make a complete list like this one; instead, just mark each event as it occurs in the question with a number in the margin. Then write the list describing each event, assigning to each the same number you wrote in the margin. That way, if you have to reread the question to check whether you've described an event accurately, you can easily find the place you need in the question itself.

If you check the above list, you will see that it reveals something interesting about the usual, seemingly complex exam question: It isn't really a single, long, complex, seemingly impenetrable story after all. Rather, it's a number of short, simple events and facts rolled into one (but easily separated). If you spot all the events and identify the issues they suggest, the battle is almost won.

Once you finish your second, slow reading, you should understand the facts and how they relate to each other. Many students make the serious mistake of failing to "get" the flow of the question. That's dangerous because you can't analyze or state the correct rule if you haven't recorded in your mind everything that's happened. If you fall into this trap, you'll appear to lack one of the fundamental skills being tested: comprehensive reading and analysis under serious time pressure. This is the same skill that is most essential to success in the practice of law. That's why law school exams are a fairly good barometer of basic legal skills.

An Interim Step: Reread Your Course Outline

You should read the question again—a third time. But before this third reading, you should review the course outline you wrote when you started the exam. By glancing again at this material, you'll cue yourself to notice any material facts or issues you may have missed on your previous run-throughs.

The Third Reading

Now reread the question, reading slowly. On this reading, make sure that you haven't missed any material events, you've taken into account all the facts surrounding each event, and you've identified all the "trigger" words.

For instance, look at the fourth material event of our sample question: "Daniel runs to bank and attempts robbery." The last sentence in the question tells you that Daniel didn't, in fact, succeed in robbing the bank; he fled without any money—thus, the event is described in the above list as Daniel's *attempted* robbery, not his *completed* robbery.

Remember, one of your tasks on this third reading is to identify and highlight (or circle) all the "trigger" words. Trigger words are adjectives, adverbs, and any other descriptive qualifiers. While professors occasionally include material that is intended to inject humor, you should always assume that each fact, funny or not, has a specific purpose. In the sample question, for example, you're told that Andy is a college senior. Why did the question include that fact? One reason may be to tell you Andy isn't an idiot or a child, which eliminates an argument that may have occurred to you when you read that he was playing with a toy gun—a possible incapacity argument.

Later, the facts state, "Carl, an off-duty cop, and his wife, Ellen." You're given specific information about the relationship between Carl and Ellen. Why? The question didn't have to include that fact, so why did it? Because the question wanted to tell you that Ellen isn't a mere acquaintance—she's Carl's wife. Why is that fact important? It suggests a reason for Ellen's fear and apprehension. As the wife of a policeman, she would be naturally more apprehensive of potential violence than would a mere acquaintance who might be walking with Carl. Also, as his wife, she might be close beside him, holding his hand perhaps.

Watch closely for words such as "immediately," "accidentally," "quickly," "recklessly," "severely," and "finally";

they each tell you something. Any time your professor uses a term that is suggestive or descriptive, be alert to the possibility that it's also important. Ask yourself why the word or phrase is included. Again, while it may be inserted as a red herring or as a touch of humor, your immediate judgment should be that every trigger word is meaningful; therefore, you should circle or highlight it. By doing so, you'll be sure to incorporate it into your answer later on, if it becomes appropriate.

You should also note any "DDTs" (dates, distances, and times) in each question, such as "ten years ago," "two hours later," and "ten feet away." Each could be the key to causation and statute-of-limitation problems, among others. Again, professors rarely include these bits of information unless they're relevant. As with all "trigger" words, you should circle or highlight dates, times, and distances.

⑥ **STEP 6: List the Material Events**

After completing your third reading, review your list of the material events in the question (which you've written in your margin). Again, here are the material events for the sample question:

❶ Andy has toy gun.
❷ Andy shoots Carl in presence of Ellen.
❸ Carl shoots Andy.
❹ Daniel takes toy gun, believing it's real.
❺ Daniel runs to bank and attempts robbery.
❻ Daniel accidentally fires Farley's gun, killing Gordon.
❼ Daniel fires toy gun and then Farley's gun at Farley, killing Farley.
❽ Police Officer Malloy fires at and misses Daniel, but shoots and kills teller Iris.

On a multi-issue question with a complex fact pattern, such as the one in the sample (most exam questions are like this), you need to list only the material events, and there are likely to be quite a few. If, however, you have a question that has only one or two issues, but on which each issue has many theoretical possibilities, you should include in your list not only the events but all of the theoretical possibilities.

For instance, in a Torts exam question on product liability, you may have only two material events: the malfunction of a product and the resulting injuries. But these events could result in a number of claims, each based on a different principle—negligence, strict product liability, breach of the implied warranty of merchantability, and so on. Also, each claim may be available against a number of parties with different interests and different defenses—the manufacturer, the distributor, the wholesaler, and the retailer. Even though the question contains only two material events, you may be called upon to discuss all these potential issues, and your list should include every one that falls under the call of the question and the professor's instructions. In other words, your list has to respond to the issues raised by the question.

If the facts of a question are particularly complex, it may help you to create a short outline of the facts themselves. This is particularly useful for Contracts and Property exam questions, where the fact pattern typically contains many transactions involving the same contract or piece of property, especially if the timing of the transactions is an issue.

⑦ **STEP 7: For a Complex, Multi-Party Question, Create an Issue-Spotting Grid**

If the fact pattern is complex, as in many Contracts, Torts, or Criminal Law questions, it's a good idea to make an issue-spotting grid that illustrates the relationships among the parties or their actions. This will help you avoid missing any issues. Remember, if you don't spot the issues, you can't discuss them, so overlooking issues is probably the biggest mistake you can make. The grid that follows is an example of an issue-spotting grid, based on the sample question.

The grid covers each person who was involved as perpetrator, victim, or potential victim in the facts and events recited in the sample question. Each square contains the basis for possible liability between the two connected parties.

When you prepare a grid during an exam, you may want to compare your class topic outline with the facts in the question in order to identify the issues. For instance, assume that in Criminal Law you've memorized a course mnemonic covering all the basic crimes— Battery, Assault, Attempt, Conspiracy, Solicitation, Accomplices, Unlawful Imprisonment, Murder, Manslaughter, Rape, Kidnapping, Perjury, Extortion, Larceny, Burglary, Embezzlement, False Pretenses, Arson, Robbery, Malicious Mischief, Forgery, and

Victim \ Δ	A	C	D
A	X	Att'd homicide Battery	Robbery Larceny
C	Assault Battery	X	Assault
D			X
E	Assault		
F			Assault Homicide
G			Homicide
M			
I			Homicide
Bank patrons			Assault, False Impris.
Bank			

Receiving Stolen Property. You could write down the components in the mnemonic and then compare them to the facts in the question, inserting the appropriate component into the corresponding square.

If you follow this method of relating your outline and mnenomics to the facts in each question, it will be just about impossible for you to miss the relevant issues.

⑧ **STEP 8: Budget Your Time on Each Question**

It's critical that you work on each question only for the time you have allotted to that question. Remember, too, that you must also budget your time among the issues in that question, or you may find yourself in trouble. For example, if you were answering the sample question, you could easily work the entire 57 minutes allocated for that question without ever reaching the killings of Farley and Iris—two out of the seven material events in the question. If you did that, your grade would suffer measurably. To avoid this result, you should use the following exam strategy.

First, make a list of the issues you intend to write on. Then, fix the amount of time you'll spend on each issue. The best way to do this is to consult your issue grid so you don't forget or overlook an essential issue. Remember, not all issues are equal. In the sample question, for example, the larceny of the gun by Daniel won't be worth as much as his killing of Farley. Because your professor will undoubtedly allocate more points to them, it's important to recognize the "bigger" issues.

How do you identify the bigger issues? The best indicator of the relative importance of issues is the amount of time your professor spent on them in class. For example, he will almost certainly have spent more time on homicide than on larceny, so you can generally assume that if a question covers both larceny and homicide, the homicide issues will be worth more points than those dealing with larceny. Secondly, look at the number of facts in the question that deal with each issue. If you're given more facts on a given issue than on the others, that issue obviously looms larger in the professor's mind and should get more of your time. For example, the battery upon Carl is open-and-shut; Daniel's culpability for Malloy's killing of Iris, on the other hand, is more complicated and requires more attention, and, therefore, more time.

Time allotment is one area in which practicing on old exams really pays off. If you practice, you'll gain experience in making better use of your time. You will be impressed, after a while, with your growing ability to fix the time you need for each issue, and especially with your ability to handle all the issues within the time span you assigned to them when you first began to write.

⑨ STEP 9: Writing Your Answer

Once you've developed your grid, chart, or list of material facts and issues and budgeted your time, you're ready to begin writing. Address each fact or issue consecutively and in "chronological" order—that is, the order in which it appears in the question. However, if the call of the question or the professor's instructions mandates a different order, by all means, use that order instead. The critical task, always, is to give the professor what she asks for.

For each material event, you should determine first how many possible issues are involved. Issues can be issues of fact or issues of law. For example, in the sample question, the first material event involves two possible sources of issues: Andy's actions as they affect Carl and his actions as they affect Ellen. For Carl, there are two possible issues of law: assault and battery. For Ellen, there's only one possible issue—assault—but there's also a factual issue: whether or not Ellen was close enough to Carl to create a reasonable apprehension of injury. If you created a decision tree of this issue (which you probably wouldn't actually do on an exam), it would look like this:

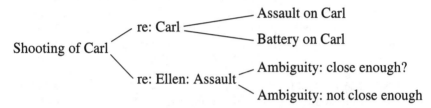

Shooting of Carl
- re: Carl
  - Assault on Carl
  - Battery on Carl
- re: Ellen: Assault
  - Ambiguity: close enough?
  - Ambiguity: not close enough

In your answer, discuss one prong of this decision tree at a time, from top to bottom. For instance, for the "Shooting of Carl" event, start by discussing whether the shooting constituted an assault on Carl. Discuss the facts as they confirm or do not confirm an assault (do this in the I-R-A-C format, discussed below), applying all the elements of assault to the facts, and then state your conclusion. After you've done that, go back to the first fork ("re: Carl") and proceed to the next branch, "Battery on Carl." Discuss this branch (again, in I-R-A-C format), and then go on to the second fork: "re: Ellen—Assault." Go to the first branch, which raises the ambiguity implicit in Ellen's position—was she close enough to Carl to justify a reasonable apprehension of imminent harm? The second branch of this fork raises the same basic issue and forces you, once again, to examine the facts in the question closely.

Creating a decision tree is very helpful when you are faced with splits of authority. Consider the following decision tree for Malloy's killing of Iris:

Malloy's killing of Iris
- some jur: felony murder
- other jur: justifiable homicide

If you had drawn this decision tree, you'd discuss the felony murder issue first (in I-R-A-C format) in accordance with the first branch— that is, for those jurisdictions that would consider this killing felony murder—then, you'd go on to the second branch and discuss the same facts for those jurisdictions that would consider the killing justifiable.

When isolating an issue, make sure you marshal all the facts bearing on that issue. This will be most difficult when the relevant facts are scattered throughout the question. Be sure you list all the facts that could possibly have relevance. For example, in dealing with Daniel's actions at the bank, you need to list the fact that he had what seemed to be a gun; he threatened both patrons and tellers; he demanded Farley's gun; he set Farley's gun off accidently; he killed Gordon; he shot at Farley with his toy gun and then with Farley's gun, killing Farley; Officer Malloy tried to shoot Daniel, but shot and killed Iris instead; and, finally, Daniel fled the bank without getting any money. These are all facts that are relevant to Daniel's liability.

If you don't see an issue clearly, don't create it. Never discuss an issue that isn't raised by the facts of the question, even if the professor spent a lot of time on it in class, and even if you're prepared to write beautifully about it. You may be surprised to find, for example, that there is no question on your Contracts exam that even remotely addresses an offeree's reliance on the offeror's promise, even though your professor may have spent a great deal of time discussing promissory estoppel. So be it! You'll get absolutely no points for writing, "Although there is no promissory estoppel issue on these facts, the issue would arise if the facts were changed slightly, as follows. . . ." As you'll recall from the discussion of the "key" method of grading, an issue that doesn't appear on the exam receives no points. If you write about it, you're wasting valuable time that could be spent earning critical points.

To summarize the issues you should discuss on your exam:

Material Facts and Events

These are the wellspring of issues. You must identify every material fact and event in the question. Any good reader with reasonable comprehension skills should be able to spot these.

As a law student with months of experience reading the facts of cases and reviewing model question and answer sources, this should be the easiest part of your exam preparation. If you still find it difficult as you face the exam, read several questions in your professor's most recent exam and list the facts and events in each. If you've already done that and still need more rehearsal, most commercial study aids have sample questions. Ask your school's academic support professional for advice on which ones to use.

Multifaceted Legal Issues

A particular fact or event can give rise to several possible solutions. This is because there may be more than one rule or theory that can be applied to the facts. In the sample question, for example, the facts concerning Malloy's killing of Iris could be construed either as unjustified felony murder or as a justifiable killing committed by Malloy in self-defense. Similarly, in questions containing fact patterns based on insanity, several possible issues may arise. This is also possible where the facts in a Torts question can be interpreted as proof either of contributory negligence or of comparative negligence.

Multifaceted Facts or Events

Sometimes, the facts themselves can be capable of several interpretations, as in questions turning on issues of intent. In these cases, it's essential to discuss both interpretations so that the professor will know that you recognize the issues.

Ambiguities

Ambiguities can arise when the facts themselves are not sufficiently well-defined to enable you to apply a rule or principle conclusively. In the example, the facts surrounding Ellen's perception of the risk to herself are ambiguous. Often, the professor intends the ambiguity. He wants to force you to see the facts in several lights, all of which he wants you to discuss. Occasionally, he may actually fail to see the ambiguity. In either case, you look good if you spot it, discuss it, and try to resolve it.

The I-R-A-C Format

By the time you take your exams, you should be well acquainted with the I-R-A-C format. "I-R-A-C" is a mnemonic for the words Issue, Rule, Analysis, and Conclusion. Exam success is dependent on how well you spot and handle issues. Mastery of those skills will give you the greatest number of points on your exam. As the above discussion emphasized, if you don't spot an issue, you can't discuss it, and you'll lose both the points your professor assigned for spotting it and the points assigned for discussing it. If you manage to isolate and identify all the major issues, you should earn at least a "C." But issue spotting alone will not earn you an "A" or "B"; you must also display your mastery over the other portions of I-R-A-C mnemonic: **R**ule, **A**nalysis, and **C**onclusion.

This book discussed the I-R-A-C formula in Chapter 4 as it applied to brief writing. If you followed the suggestions there, you are familiar with the format and understand how useful it can be in analyzing exam questions. You will also appreciate how one application in the approach to first-year strategies and tactics can be used again and again.

After you've spotted and stated an issue, turn to the second element of I-R-A-C: stating the applicable rule. There are several things to keep in mind about stating the rule.

State the Rule Completely

Even when you're sure that an exam question deals only with some, but not all, aspects of a rule, state the entire rule. If you state the entire rule, you won't overlook any elements that may be lurking in the facts. If you state only that part of the rule that you consider to be relevant, there's a possibility you will overlook an element your professor intended you to cover (and thus lose points). The crime of larceny, for instance, has four elements: 1) a trespassory taking, 2) and a carrying away or asportation, 3) of the personal property of another, 4) with the intent to steal. Although the taking may be the most important single element, they're all essential. If you don't state the entire rule, you may overlook the fact that the question contains no evidence of an intent to steal—hence, no larceny. If you do state every element of the rule, you won't make that mistake.

State the Rule Accurately

When you state a rule, you must be sure that you get it right. Murder, for example, is not "an unlawful, intentional killing." If you state the rule that simply and inaccurately, you will be omitting the essential element, "with malice aforethought." That element can be satisfied by either an intentional act or by conduct that is "reckless" or evidences "an extreme indifference to the value of human life." Similarly, criminal battery is not "an intentional touching causing injury," it's the "unlawful application of force to the person of another resulting either in bodily injury or an offensive touching." In short, you won't receive any points for stating a legal rule if you don't state it correctly. Worse still, if you state a rule incorrectly, you may end up either discussing an issue that isn't in the question at all or missing an issue that is present. If you've prepared by using the methods in this book, you've been memorizing rules throughout the course and should know them well enough to state them. Conscientious preparation is the only way to ensure you'll state the rules accurately when you're under the pressure of the exam.

You Don't Have to State the Same Rule Twice for the Same Question

Note that the issues of "robbery" and "murder" arise more than once in the model answer; the rules for each remain the same, however, so they need to be stated only once—preferably the first time each issue occurs. When writing your answer, remember that your professor will grade your answer to any single question in one sitting; therefore, you need not repeat all the elements of a rule so long as your first statement of it clearly indicates that you know the rule and when to apply it.

You Don't Have to Name Cases

As a general rule, you don't need to cite cases, statutes, or any other authority. Naming them won't impress the professor, who may even wonder why you spent time memorizing case names rather than learning how to see and understand issues and apply rules to facts.

Naturally, there are exceptions. You should always cite cases if the question or professor asks you to. Also, certain cases are so identified with a rule, standard, or principle that the very name is shorthand for the rule itself (e.g., *Miranda, Palsgraf,* or *Roe v. Wade*). Note, however, that there are very few cases that rise to this level of authority. If a case name doesn't immediately spring to mind, don't worry about. So long as you remember what the case stands for, the name doesn't matter.

Be wary of the trap generated by too much reliance on the facts and names of your cases: Too much reliance may make your thinking so rigid that you immediately associate the facts in a question with a particular case without recognizing that your professor has varied the facts just enough to create different issues. Think carefully before you allow yourself to say, "Oh, those are the facts of the (*Bluto*) case." Your professor almost certainly won't write a question that mirrors precisely any case you've studied—even fact patterns based on a specific case will vary the facts in some way. If you rely on case names and deal with the facts of a question in this stilted, rigid way, you're sure to miss at least one issue. You can, of course, analogize from the facts in the question to the facts of a case you've studied, but only if you can point out both the similarities and the differences.

This advice applies especially to closed-book exams. If the exam is open book, and you need to refer to a case or statute section, by all means mention the source. Remember, though, that you *must* explain why that material is relevant; an irrelevant reference to authority is a point-losing mistake.

What to Do if You Can't Remember the Rule

Time pressure and anxiety may cause you to forget a rule. If this happens, there are three things you can do:

If You're Sure There's a Rule, but Can't Remember All the Details, Don't Panic

If you find yourself in this situation, you're experiencing a classic, temporary "mental block."

The key fact is that you know there is an applicable rule. The details will come if you don't panic and if you work hard at remembering. First, try to recall everything that's in any way associated with the contents of the rule. Use contextual clues to help you remember: Think of the place in your notes where that rule is buried, the facts of a case that may fit the rule, or the class during which the rule was discussed and what was said.

If none of this works, consider leaving a space in your answer and coming back to the question later. You've almost certainly had the experience of remembering something only after you stopped trying hard to remember it. (You see an actor on the screen in a new context and you try hard to remember his name—the more you try, the less you remember. Finally you give up, but minutes later, miraculously, his name pops suddenly to mind). This phenomenon happens because when you stop searching your memory you become relaxed, and this helps you to remember.

Finally, if you're impenetrably blocked over one question, just move on. You may find that the rule "pops" suddenly into your mind when you're thinking of something else. When it does, jot it down, go back, and fill in the blank space. Even if you don't remember the rule, at least you'll have saved the time you would have spent fruitlessly trying to remember, and you'll be less likely to panic.

You May Be Able to Back into the Rule by Thinking of the Underlying Principles

Earlier, this book discussed the importance of memorizing rationales and policies that explain or underlie each rule. Knowing these rationales and policies will help you to handle fact patterns that don't fall neatly under one rule or another. In addition, it will help you to recreate the rules you may have forgotten. If there are two competing policies and you're not sure which one applies, recreate the two rules that would result and state them both—then, discuss each one separately, in the I-R-A-C format.

You may not have noticed, but the model answer fails to identify a rule. Instead, it "fills in the blanks" and arrives at the correct conclusion by reasoning from the underlying principles of the missing rule. If you look at item 6 under "Daniel's Liability," you'll see that the answer forgot the "apparent present ability" test, which states that "attempt" requires only that there be an apparent present ability to commit the intended crime, not the actual ability. The answer did, however, mention the policy underlying the rule: to punish those who manifest their willingness to commit crimes. Thus, as the answer points out, it doesn't matter that D couldn't actually have killed F with the toy gun. By knowing the policy behind the element of attempt, the answer managed to recreate the elements of the rule.

Developing a Rule When There Isn't One

An exam question may depend on facts that suggest that there should be a rule when you can't remember one. You think long and hard, but you can't remember ever having seen or discussed a rule governing those facts. Under these circumstances, the wisest thing to do is to reason from the facts and develop the rationale for a rule that should logically apply. The facts should suggest the rationale and the rule. If they suggest two possible conflicting views or rules, develop them both. Then state one or both, reasoning from the facts as stated. That way, you will demonstrate to the professor that you understand the process and can "think like a lawyer"— that is, from facts to rationale to rule.

Never Admit That You Don't Know the Rule

Regardless of what approach you take, never admit that you can't remember or don't know the rule. If you confess that you don't know, you're telling the professor, "Deduct points here." If you create or recreate a rule based on the rationales or public policies suggested by the facts, there's a good chance that the professor will congratulate you for thinking through the process. Remember, a professor spends an average of four minutes grading an exam answer. If you don't acknowledge openly that you don't know the law, you may cover up your lack of knowledge so well that the professor won't even see it. In the example analyzed above—D's attempted murder of F with the toy gun—it's highly unlikely that a professor would deduct many (if any) points for the student's failure to state the "apparent present ability" rule because the answer displays an understanding of the underlying rationale so well.

Analysis

It is in the "A" or "analysis" portion of I-R-A-C that you can shine and raise your grade above the average. This is where you demonstrate your problem-solving skills—the skills that generally separate the top students from the rest. In fact, most, if not all, professors say that this is the most important part of any exam answer. Consequently, you should spill more ink writing the analysis than in writing any other part of your answer.

Under "analysis," you explain how and why the rule you've stated applies to the facts. You must avoid a common failing: Don't announce your conclusion immediately upon the heels of the rule. Here's an example of how *not* to say it: "A criminal assault is either an attempt to commit a battery or the intentional and physical creation of fear of imminent bodily harm in the mind of the victim. Andy is liable for an assault on Carl and probably also an assault on Ellen."

That statement contains absolutely no explanation of *why* Andy's actions constitute an assault on Carl or Ellen. It is simply a conclusion without supporting analysis and would earn no points at all.

(*Caveat*: On a very short essay question—say 15 minutes long—your answer has to be precise and short, so one or two sentences of analysis may have to suffice. The time constraints will not permit a more extended analysis.)

The Basic Rule in Analysis: Divide and Conquer

In applying rules to facts, you must first divide the rule into its components or elements. If the facts suggest that a burglary has been attempted or committed, you would begin by writing down the rule governing burglary: "At common law, a burglary is the breaking and entering of a dwelling at night with the intent to commit a felony therein." If you analyze it, this rule actually consists of five individual elements or components: a breaking, an entering, a dwelling, nighttime, and felonious intent.

After you state the rule, you should examine and apply all these elements, in order, to determine which are present and which are not.

Note, though, that you don't have to discuss every element. For instance, in the sample question, consider the issue whether Daniel is guilty of larceny in taking Andy's gun. Assume that you've stated the rule defining larceny: A larceny is the trespassory taking and carrying away of personal property of another with intent to steal it. You have defined larceny as having four distinct elements: 1) a trespassory taking, 2) and a carrying away, 3) of personal property, 4) with intent to steal. You should then ask yourself if two competent lawyers, one the prosecutor and the other the defense lawyer, would be able to support reasonable opposing arguments on both sides of the issue of larceny. On the above facts, there could be no reasonable argument by the defense.

Therefore, the answer concluded that the facts would "satisfy the elements of larceny."

Now consider, instead, the issue of assault by Andy upon Ellen. The rule for assault is "a criminal assault is either an attempt to commit a battery or the intentional and physical creation of fear of imminent bodily harm in the mind of the victim." Under the facts in the example, the two imaginary opposing lawyers could certainly argue over the "mind of the victim" element. Both Ellen's perception of imminent harm to herself and the reasonableness of her perception are clearly at issue. A good answer would definitely consider both in detail. The answer should also deal with Andy's intent, which is also subject to dispute and analysis. Use all the available facts. (Just as if you were trying to win any argument—whether what restaurant to have dinner at or what band was the best band of all time.)

Some Key Words in Rules Always Require Discussion

There are many rules that incorporate words that, by their very nature, require a thorough discussion of the facts and their meaning. Words such as "reasonable," "clear," "foreseeable," and "material" are so imprecise and wide ranging as to mandate case-by-case and question-by-question interpretation. They are intended only as a guideline for your analysis. In the model answer, the answer explained that Carl was probably entitled to a claim of self-defense. In arriving at this conclusion, the answer reasoned that his shooting of Andy was a "reasonable" response to Andy's assault upon him. In arriving at this conclusion, the answer considered, described, and weighed all the facts surrounding Andy's actions and Carl's actions. You can't apply the word "reasonable" without developing all the facts and reasoning from them to your conclusion, which must be defensible in the light of the relevant rule.

Argue Both Sides

When you discuss an element or component of a rule, it's wise to present and argue from both sides. As a law student, you're being trained to perform one of the integral roles of the practitioner—to function as an advocate. To succeed as an advocate, you must know and understand both sides of a negotiation or a litigation. You can't serve your client well if you don't understand the other side's strengths and weaknesses. On an exam, you may sympathize with one side of an issue, but you must still show your professor that you understand and can articulate both.

Supplying the Missing Elements of "Close" Rules

Some fact patterns will suggest one or more of the elements of a rule, but omit one or two other essential elements. What should you do under those circumstances?

Consider Daniel's taking of Andy's gun. If you're on your toes, the facts will suggest that a robbery is involved. You know the rule: "A robbery is a larceny from the person accomplished by force or fear." Because Daniel has taken Andy's gun, the facts are "robbery-oriented." But an essential element of robbery is missing—the element of force or fear. You're torn between two choices: Should you discuss robbery at all, or skip it? You should discuss it, but make it clear that you know the whole rule and that you understand that the rule does not apply because an essential element of the crime is missing.

Knowing When to Discuss an Issue at All

Until now, this book has been discussing situations in which a rule is applicable and should be discussed. Whether or not you should discuss a rule at all will depend upon the extent to which the facts suggest the elements of the rule. Look at the sample question once again and examine whether the facts suggest a burglary as to the bank.

Common law burglary is the breaking and entering of a dwelling at night with the intent to commit a prescribed felony within the dwelling. In the fact pattern, the question has a bank, not a dwelling. You're told that it's morning and the bank is open and has lots of customers; those facts clearly negate the essential elements of "a dwelling," "breaking and entering," and "night-time." Three of the five elements of common law burglary are missing.

With so many required elements missing, you could justifiably decide not to discuss burglary at all, even though some modern

statutes do eliminate the "nighttime" and "dwelling" require-
ments. Your professor should not take any points off for this
decision because it is supported by the facts. However, if you did
choose to discuss it, you would be wise to discuss the common
law rule first, stating that the breaking, nighttime, and dwelling
elements were missing, and that no burglary was committed.
Then, you should state the modern rule but explain that the modern
rule still requires proof of the "breaking and entering" element.

If you did discuss it, you would not need to spend much time on the
issue of intent because it's clear in the facts that the necessary
intent was present.

How Much of the Fact Pattern Should You Review?

Don't repeat any part of the fact pattern verbatim. The professor
knows the facts (he created them); your professor wants to see
what you make of them. In a complicated question with many facts
leading in all directions, for each issue you find, mention only
those facts that relate to that issue. Weave the facts into your
discussion, picking up "threads" of facts only as you need them.

Resist the temptation to state more of the facts than you need for a
particular conclusion. Here's an example of an overblown fact
pattern: "Having stolen the gun from Andy, D walked into the
bank waving a gun and asked the tellers for all their money and the
customers to hit the floor. D is guilty of robbery as to the bank,
and of assault and false imprisonment as to the tellers and the
customers." The statement "having stolen the gun from Andy" is
completely irrelevant to the crimes committed by Daniel within
the bank and does not belong in this discussion.

Note that the model answer avoids the problem of discussing
irrelevant facts by separating the answer into several paragraphs,
each with its own heading. If you're comfortable with this format,
it's a good device for avoiding excessive facts. The heading
"Carl's Liability for Shooting Andy" clearly suggests which facts
you should be talking about. This format has the added benefit
of giving the professor an easy tool for checking your answer
against his answer key. It also ensures that you will seem organized. The format will make you appear logical and lawyer-like,
which may impress your professor enough to give you the

benefit of the doubt when he hesitates between an average grade and a superior one.

Never Assume Facts

Assumptions about facts are dangerous—they will only cost you points. All the facts the professor wants you to consider are on your exam. Don't re-write her question by adding facts of your own. If facts seem to be missing, you should assume that she intended to omit them and wants you to discuss the issues in light of the omissions.

For instance, on the issue of Andy's assault on Ellen, you aren't told whether or not she was close enough to Carl to create a reasonable anticipation of imminent bodily harm. Therefore, you can't make any assumptions about her proximity and you can't say, "Because Ellen was so close to Carl, she could reasonably fear imminent bodily harm." However, it is reasonable to infer from the facts that she was walking next to him, but you have to say that you're *making the inference* and then explain why it's relevant and reasonable.

Suppose that in the very first sentence of the sample question it had omitted the words "realistic-looking" when describing the toy gun. This omission would necessarily have affected your analysis of the entire question: It would be relevant to the issue of Carl's self-defense claim and to the attempted robbery and false imprisonment claims, among others. If the gun was clearly and visibly a toy, for instance, you could not reasonably find false imprisonment of the bank customers. They would have known that they were free to leave the bank and that Daniel was probably a crackpot. You would not be able to assume that a gun that was described only as a toy gun used in a game was realistic-looking if you were not told that it was. Under those circumstances—the absence of a clear description—you'd be wise to argue the facts in the alternative—that is, what would happen, on the one hand, if the gun looked like a real gun, and, on the other hand, if the gun was clearly not real.

Take the Facts at Face Value

Draw whatever issues you can from the facts, but don't "question" the integrity of the facts as stated. For instance, in the sample question, you were told that Andy was unconscious when Daniel took the gun. Accept and reason from that fact; don't say to yourself, "What would happen if, in fact, Andy was conscious. . . ." There are enough facts and issues to analyze without adding your own. It's a waste of time to create facts and issues that aren't there.

Don't Cut Your Analysis Short

Occasionally, you'll face an exam question in which a single issue is so dominant that it seems to dispose of all other issues.

Suppose, for example, that a Torts question asks you to discuss only intentional torts, and you conclude that the principal actor in the fact pattern lacks intent. You may be tempted to say, "Because X didn't act intentionally, he is not liable," and stop there. While this may be adequate for a lawyer in "real life," it won't do as an exam answer. Instead, you have to use the "but if" method of analysis—that is, "On these facts, X probably didn't act intentionally, but if he had, he would be liable for. . . ."

Here's another example: In a Contracts exam, when you're deciding the rights and liabilities of the two parties to a contract, you will have to analyze each of the following: does a contract exist, has it been performed by both parties, was it breached by one party or both, what defenses are available, and what remedies apply? If you come to the conclusion that there was no meeting of the minds and therefore no contract, you may be tempted to stop at that point. Don't. You need to go further. You might write, "There was no meeting of the minds. But if there had been a meeting of the minds and a contract, the contract was breached by Party A, which failed to perform in. . . ."

This is somewhat related to the above caveat about not assuming facts. In the sample question, you will remember, it wasn't clear whether or not Ellen was close enough to Carl to justify holding Andy liable for an assault on her, but you wouldn't simply say, "From these facts, we can conclude that Ellen was close enough to justify a finding of assault. . . ." Instead, you might say, "It appears reasonable to assume from the circumstances that Ellen was close enough to justify a finding of assault, but if we assume for our discussion that she wasn't, then. . . ."

Be Wary of "Inspirations"

You may think you've spotted a "glimmer" issue on your exam, one you think everyone else has missed; you may see a new issue for which you have a unique and novel analysis never before advanced, or you may suddenly be inspired by a concept that will prove a prevailing doctrine wrong. If you're like most people, you'll be tempted to display your new erudition at length. Resist the temptation. If you must succumb to the temptation to do it, confine your remarks to a few quick observations, or wait until you've finished the exam and looked it over carefully. As discussed previously, performing well on the exam means spotting and correctly analyzing every issue. An "A" answer, as the model illustrates, doesn't have to propose a novel argument or even contain any flashes of brilliance. The place for displaying your command of the "cutting edge of the law" is Law Review or another student journal, not your first-year exams.

You Must Draw a Conclusion

You may find drawing conclusions very difficult. It's a skill that's at odds with what you did during class. Class discussions almost never result in a conclusion; instead, you discuss arguments for both sides, and you move on. On exams, however, you must draw your own conclusions.

The important thing to remember, though, is that you don't necessarily have to come to the correct conclusion. You'll do fine so long as you draw a reasonable and logical conclusion that is consistent with all the facts. In the example, Daniel's liability for Malloy's shooting of Iris turns on the circumstances under which the incident took place. In some jurisdictions, Daniel would be liable even though he did not himself shoot Iris; in others, he wouldn't be. If you state both possibilities in your answer, it doesn't mean you haven't come to a conclusion that firmly adopts one over the other. Rather, it shows that you recognize that there are two different but equally valid conclusions under the same facts, depending on the jurisdiction.

When There Are Two Ways of Resolving a Discussion, Pick the One Your Professor Would Prefer

It's simply human nature to view someone who agrees with you as more intelligent and well informed than someone who doesn't. While you may not actually agree with your professor, and while an exam that otherwise deserves an "A" certainly won't be downgraded if you show your disagreement, the impact of agreeing with her when the opportunity arises can have a subtle positive and salutary effect.

In Chapter 3, Drawing a Bead on Your Professor, this book discussed the importance of understanding your professor's views. On an exam question, if you know your professor's position on an issue, and if you can resolve that issue as your professor would resolve it, you should do so. Try to end your discussion with the view your professor prefers, and then (if you reasonably can) state that this is the better view.

When the Conclusion Contradicts Policy and Rationale Concerns

Sometimes the strict application of a rule to the facts will create a ridiculous result. If this happens to you on an exam, proceed with your usual strict application of the rule. Then, when you reach the absurd conclusion, say, "But the underlying policy and rationale concerns behind the rule tell us that the rule was never intended to operate this way" and proceed to explain what the result ought to be when you apply the "spirit" of the law.

Tips on Implementing These Test-Taking Strategies

Don't Over-Outline Your Answer Before You Write It

The standard line is that a student should spend a third of his time writing an outline of the answer before he begins to write.
The traditional wisdom is that you should plan every line before writing, expanding on your outline by filling in the blanks when you write your answer.

Instead of this standard approach, as explained above, you should simply identify the material facts and issues, and then to proceed directly with your answer. Here are the main reasons for advocating this approach.

Your Grade Depends on the Contents of Your Exam Answer

You want to get as many words into your answer as you possibly can. If you don't write anything until you've used up a third of your time for any question, you limit the amount you can write. You won't receive any points for your beautiful and thorough outline—only for the material you put down in your answer.

The Time Pressure

The time pressure during exams makes it unrealistic to spend one-third of the total time in outlining your answers. Especially with complex, issue-laden exams in subjects like Torts, Contracts, and Criminal Law, the battle is won by identifying as many issues as you can and then writing about them with as much detail as you can manage in the short time you're given.

"Over-Outlining" Results in Writing Everything Twice

If you outline in detail and then reproduce and extend that outline into your answer, you're simply taking the time to write everything twice. This is obviously non-productive. The time is much better spent writing an extensive answer—one time. You can develop the technique of thinking and writing at the same time. Everyone does this when they have to, and you'll be able to do it during your exam, too. It's not necessary to do all of your thinking and organizing before you start to write.

A Question-by-Question Outline Isn't Really Necessary

The purpose of outlining is to ensure that your answer is organized, and the purpose of an organized answer is threefold: 1) to guarantee that you don't miss any issues; 2) to ensure that you offer the rule, analysis, and conclusion for every issue; and 3) to convey to your professor that you have an orderly, lawyer-like mind. If you undertake the bare-bones "material facts and issues" outlining suggested in this chapter, you'll accomplish these three tasks while spending no more than 20 percent of your time preparing your answer before you write. You'll have the best of both worlds: an organized answer, plus the maximum amount of time to write it.

Don't Address Issues Out of Order

Don't jump around from issue to issue. It will make it much harder for the professor to measure and grade your answer (think back to the sample answer key). If you were given the sample question on an exam, you may be tempted to deal first with Daniel's liability for Malloy's shooting of Iris because it's a "big" issue.

However, if you treat issues out of order, you'll be more likely to overlook other earlier issues. As discussed in the answer-key method of grading, that would cost you a lot of points. As stated above, taking issues out of order will make it more difficult for the professor to grade your exam because everyone else is likely to address the issues in order and she will view your answer as an inroad on her time and methods. It's not a good idea to irritate anyone who has so much control over your grades and, perhaps, your destiny.

Don't Let Your Emotions Get the Better of You

When you're a lawyer, it will be important for you to maintain your independent professional judgment even when you feel strongly about an issue. For example, if a friend or relative of yours is killed during a bank hold-up, you may feel difficulty and reluctance in defending a person accused of bank robbery. Similarly, in answering the sample question, you may instinctively recoil from Daniel's actions and may fail to see a potentially valid defense. You can't afford to do this in real life or on the exam. You must learn to keep your emotions and your personal prejudices out of it. You must also keep your political and religious beliefs from influencing your answer.

Don't Write Anything Personal on Your Exam

If you have something to say to the professor that concerns you personally and not the substance of the exam, see him during office hours. Don't, for example, write, "I've been playing a lot of tennis and my hand is sore. Sorry my handwriting is so awful, I'm doing my best." Why call attention to your problem when the professor may not notice it? Or he may think, "Why would a student deliberately hurt her chances on the exam by making it impossible to write well?" Apologetic or ingratiating notes won't win you points; they'll just make you look unprofessional and will diminish your professor's impression of you and your exam.

Don't Fool Around

Some professors spend a great deal of time creating questions that are either humorous in themselves or that suggest a humorous answer. You may be tempted to display your ability to bring a smile to her lips. For example, you may have been tempted to begin your answer to the sample question with, "Well, if it isn't another shoot-out at the O.K. Corral."

Resist the temptation to be humorous. Even if your professor includes some humor, she generally does so for a purpose: Using unusual names for people and places is often a professor's way of preventing students from confusing the names. You have no comparable reason to joke or play around. If you inject your own humor, she may think that you're attempting to camouflage your lack of organization and poor exam-writing skills, so avoid it. Plus, humor is dangerous—what may seem funny to you may seem completely inappropriate or offensive to your professor.

Keep Yourself Out of Your Answer

Keep your answer objective and impersonal. There's nothing to be gained by writing, "I think . . . ," or "In my opinion. . . ." Your answer obviously reflects your thought process. It's unnecessary and unprofessional to suggest that the right answers are unique to you. Also, the use of these phrases makes you look tentative and unsure of your answer.

Forget Your High School and College Essay Style

In high school and college, you were taught to write complex essays using an introduction, topic sentences, summaries, transition sentences, and the like. On law school exams, this type of organization only wastes time. Notice that the model answer is completely free of these devices, namely because they're unnecessary. (For the same reason, don't waste time giving the history of a rule or principle.) Your professor will grant points only for a clear statement of the issues you identify, the rules that apply, the analyses you provide, and the conclusions you reach. He won't add points for an introduction that summarizes all the major points. It will only be repetitive, and it will waste valuable time for both of you.

Don't Construct Your Answer in the "Question-and-Answer" Style

In the model answer, each new topic starts with a simple header indicating what issue or facts the section will discuss—for example, "Andy's Liability for Shooting Carl." If, instead, you began that section, "Is A Liable for Shooting C?" you'd have to waste time and space in answering your own question— "Yes, A is liable for shooting C." It's better just to avoid the question-and-answer approach in the first place.

Use a Straightforward, Simple, Crisp Writing Style

Law students—and lawyers—often have a cumbersome, leaden, and convoluted writing style. They think they have to distinguish themselves by avoiding the simple style of novelists and journalists. In any event, you're not Oliver Wendell Holmes—at least not yet—and you're not writing for posterity. Avoid interlocking principal and subordinate clauses. Avoid unnecessary and extraneous verbiage. There are few thoughts that cannot be expressed in one simple declarative sentence. As you write your exam, think of yourself as a salesperson or TV journalist who has exactly 60 seconds to get her point across. Above all, make it easy for your professor to pierce your language and reach your thoughts.

Making Up for a Time-Allocation Blunder

Imagine you're working on a 60-minute question. You look at your watch and are shocked to discover that you have five minutes left. You realize you've covered only five of the seven critical issues. What should you do?

No matter what, you must put the question aside when you reach your 60-minute limit. NEVER, under any circumstances, violate your per-question time allocation. This can't be stressed enough. You'll be very tempted to break it, but if you do, the results will be disastrous. You will think, "I know that with just ten extra minutes, I can write a world-beating answer to this question. I'll just knock a few minutes off each of the other questions." Here are three iron-clad reasons why you should never do this.

You May Be Throwing Away Big Points on Later Questions

If you spend too much time on an early question, you'll have less time for the later ones. You may very well panic when you actually get to those later questions and lose your ability to analyze them in a systematic way. Remember what you learned from the answer key discussed earlier: The big points come from the basics—spotting issues and analyzing them. If you spend too much time on an early question, you will end up getting lost among the many smaller and less important issues of the later questions, forfeiting the "big" points. It's just not worth it.

You Will Be Showing a Lack of One of the Fundamental Skills of a Lawyer

One of the most important skills you will need as a lawyer is the ability to work under severe time pressure. You'll never have as much time to devote to a project as you would like. And many projects will be competing for your attention at the same time—in the very same way as competing exam questions. Your first-year exams require the same time-management skills as a law practice. When you spend too much time on a single question, you're only proving that you haven't yet developed the ability to organize your time in the way the professor anticipates.

You and your classmates are all under identical time pressure. If you don't demonstrate your ability to deal with that pressure as well as some others, you don't deserve a superior grade.

A Great First Answer Will Not Cancel Out an Inferior Later One

When you yield to the pressure and spend too much time on your first answer, you may delude yourself into thinking that if you spend the additional time, your professor will be so impressed that he will recognize you as another Benjamin Cardozo and overlook the fact that you failed to answer the key issues on a later question. As stated above, that won't happen because professors just don't grade that way. They grade each answer separately. They read, measure, and grade the entire class's answers to question #1; then, to question #2; and so on. Each answer is graded relatively, against your classmates' answers to the same question. By the time the professor gets to your third answer, he will probably have forgotten that it was you who wrote that brilliant answer to question #1. If you write an A answer on the first question, a B answer on the second, a C answer on the third, and a D answer on the fourth, you won't get an A on the exam—even if your first answer was good enough for Law Review.

What Should You Do When You Have Five Minutes Left for a Question

Here's the scene—you look at your watch, you have five minutes left, and you're not going to allow yourself to run over. What do you do? Write as short a summary or synopsis of the rest of the answer as you possibly can to show your professor that you recognize the issues but have had to condense your answer to stay within your self-imposed schedule. In one sentence, state the issue and the appropriate rule. Then, in no more than three short sentences, give your analysis and a simple conclusion. Use as few words as possible, and race through. If you do this, you may not get the maximum number of points, but you'll get some.

Never write "OUT OF TIME" in big letters across the page or confess that you ran out of time. Since that may not be apparent to your professor, there's no advantage in "confessing." Remember, the ability to work under time pressure is one of the skills you're supposed to be demonstrating. Telling the professor outright that you can't do this is like shouting that you have not yet learned to function "like a lawyer." This is something you definitely want to avoid.

Curing Major Mistakes in Your Answer

Sometimes even the best students find that they've made a major blunder: on review, they find that they have totally misread the facts, applied the wrong rule, or the like. If you follow this book's system completely, you're unlikely ever to find yourself in this position. If you do, however, stop where you are, acknowledge your mistake ("I realize now that I have misinterpreted the facts" or "I wish to change my conclusion" or "I have misstated the parol evidence rule"), and proceed as quickly as you can with the correct answer. Don't assume that the professor will not have spotted your mistake; if you've said something like, "Negligence requires intent," and you don't correct yourself but go on to analyze the issues under this erroneous statement of the basic concept of negligence, your professor can't give you any points even though your subsequent analysis of the facts under your misstated rule may be logical.

What to Do if You Finish Early

If you finish early, congratulations! But you're not done yet! Don't get up and turn in your exam. It's generally a good idea to resist the temptation to leave. Use the extra time to review your answers. But don't invent new issues where none exist or trip yourself up in some other way. It's an especially good idea to stay until the end if your professor is the proctor because she may be asked by another student to clarify some obscure fact or issue. You want to be there when she does. Your professor's answer may lead you to make a vital change in a section of your exam.

Should You Type Your Exam?

The short answer is "yes." Typing looks more professional, you will be able to quickly and neatly edit any mistakes or omissions in your answer, and you'll be able to get more information down. Sometimes, students make the mistake of choosing to handwrite exams because they believe this forces them to slow down and think more; keep in mind, though, that you're going to be under intense time pressure—anything that will slow you down should be avoided at all costs. If you are not a good typist or have never taken an exam on a computer before, use old exam questions or commercial study aid questions to practice.

If you are typing your exams, your school will make you download a program that will block you from accessing other programs, information, or the Internet while you are taking your exam. Make sure you pay attention to any e-mails or other communication regarding this, as you will likely have to download it to your computer far in advance of the actual exams. (For many schools, if you miss the deadline, you're going to be stuck handwriting the exam.) Also, make sure you make yourself thoroughly accustomed to the program before you sit down for your exams. While all of these programs are similar to commonly used word-processing programs, many of them do not have some of the features you may have come to rely on (e.g., a spell-check function).

If You Really Want to Use a Bluebook, Write Neatly

Theoretically, a professor grading an exam should ignore irrelevant obstacles such as bad grammar, misspellings, and sloppy handwriting. They are irrelevant because they don't prove anything about the student's ability to reason and comprehend. But, realistically, it's virtually impossible for a professor to avoid being influenced (negatively) by a bluebook that's riddled with cross-outs, misspelled words, grammatical errors, or illegible words and phrases. You can never be sure that your professor will not grade you down for a messy bluebook.

Also, a lot of crossed-out words and sentences may lead your professor to think that you're either indecisive or unsure of your analysis. You can't do much to improve your spelling or your grammar—although you're foolish not to have been working at improving them during your school year—but you can make a conscious effort to control your handwriting. You should make a special effort to write neatly, even under the time constraints. Print, if that helps, and if you can print fast enough. Always write in ink, not pencil. Ink looks more professional, is easier to read, and is less likely to smear. (Although, if you're left-handed, make sure you're careful in your choice of pens.) If you know that you tend to cross out a lot, consider using erasable ink or correction fluid on your exams.

Use Abbreviations

Abbreviating names in your answer saves time. Look at the model answer: All of the characters' names were abbreviated after the first use. You may want to abbreviate place names and causes of actions as well. Be certain, though, that you identify the abbreviations the first time you use them and, especially, that each one is distinct from the others. Also, make sure that you identify abbreviations again in each new question, since your professor (or grader) may not be able to read your entire exam at once.

Limit yourself to easily understandable abbreviations for parties, causes of action, and places. Don't incorporate your own personal system of shorthand, even if you've developed an especially handy one for taking notes during class. Don't use any more abbreviations than necessary, and never use unusual or unconventional abbreviations. These will only cost you points when your professor has to spend time "decoding" what you wrote. Remember, the last thing you want to do is annoy the professor who grades your answer.

Different Types of Exam Questions

So far, this discussion has focused on the most common type of first-year exam question: the multi-party, multi-transaction recitation of hypothetical facts, events, and issues. This type of question tests your ability to analyze the facts, to spot issues, to recognize and cite the correct rule, and to reach logical conclusions by weighing the facts and the rules. (This is the format used in Bar Exam essay questions, as well.)

You should know, however, that there are occasional variations on this theme. These are better suited to some classes than to others. In Civil Procedure, for example, a question may consist of a single, very long fact pattern. The parties make various motions as the facts are developed, and you're asked to decide how each motion should be resolved. On a Property exam, you may face a question describing various transactions, all or some of which relate to a particular piece of property; and you are asked to describe the rights of each party to the transactions. These questions all test the same basic skills as the usual hypothetical question, although they do differ somewhat from the sample question.

Pure Policy/Evaluation Questions

Occasionally, as in a subject like Constitutional Law, a professor may aim a question at a higher level of skill, comprehension, and competence by focusing on problems that call for intellectual skills beyond problem solving.

Your professor may provide a quote for you to explain. For example, your professor may give you this quote: "Without the aid of the doctrine a patient who received permanent injuries of a serious character, obviously the result of someone's negligence, would be unable to recover unless the doctors and nurses in attendance voluntarily chose to disclose the identity of the negligent person and the facts establishing liability." In that case, you should identify the quote and where it's from (if you can) and then explain what area of law it is dealing with. Here, you should identify the quote as being from *Ybarra v. Spangard*, explain that it is the leading case applying the doctrine of *res ipsa* to medical malpractice cases, and then explain the rules and policies behind the doctrine itself.

Your professor may also ask you to evaluate a proposed law or issue. For instance, you may be asked: Under what circumstances should a person be subject to mandatory drug testing? Or you may be asked to decide a case in which mandatory drug testing is the central legal issue—if you were a judge, how would you rule? In answering this question, you will have to display your ability to resolve conflicting legal and social interests and to apply seemingly contradictory rules in an unsettled area of the law. (Society constantly faces issues of these kinds—legalized abortion, affirmative action, assisted suicide, control of expression on the Internet.) This requires greater social maturity and intellectual acuity than does basic problem solving. However, because it's more difficult to consistently grade a question of this kind, it's rare for professors to ask questions of this type.

Taking Objective Exams

Objective exams, whether multiple-choice or true-false, test a skill fundamentally different from the skills tested on hypothetical essay exams. Essay questions require you to recall spontaneously all the rules you've learned—the facts may suggest the applicable rule, but they won't supply it or apply it for you. You must know and understand the rule yourself, and you must decide when and how to apply it. In an objective exam, you are given the correct answer. You have only to recognize it from a group of four possibilities, three of which are incorrect.

What makes an objective exam tricky, though, is that you have to remember and recognize lots of details, not only broad concepts. As discussed in Chapter 7, Test Preparation, this will affect the way you study for the exam. It will probably be more helpful to memorize mnemonics and other shortcuts to recall all of the individual elements of rules than to develop and use a course outline. Even so, it is very rare for a law school exam to be completely objective—usually you'll get a multiple choice portion followed by several essays. The best way to improve your objective-exam skills is to practice and follow some of these basic strategies.

The Basic Approach: A Process of Elimination

With any objective test, the correct approach in answering multiple-choice questions is not to "reach" immediately for the right answer, but to eliminate systematically all the incorrect answers, thus leaving yourself with the correct one. You do this by considering each option consecutively and individually and deciding if it can possibly be the correct response. If it can be, mark it with a **Y** for "yes" (assuming you're permitted to make marks on the test booklet). If it cannot be correct, mark it with an **N** for "no." Ideally, you'll find only one Y answer, and it must be the correct one. (In case this doesn't happen easily, the following tips explain how to guess effectively.)

Read carefully

The easiest trap to fall into on an objective test is to read so quickly and carelessly that you "see" words in the questions that aren't actually there. Remember, an objective exam tests your grasp of details, and the details frequently turn on one word or phrase in a question. To answer correctly, you must read carefully and analytically.

If you're allowed to put marks in the test booklet, highlight important words and phrases as you read: for example, party names, dates, and critical descriptions (such as that a party is ten years old or a merchant). If the facts are complex, diagram them. You should read the entire question and all four answer options before you attempt to compare and select among the answers. This will enable you to see the whole picture and the whole range of possibilities before you concentrate consecutively on each choice.

Eliminating Answers: If Any Part Is "False" or Incorrect, the Entire Choice Is Incorrect

In an objective test on the law, an answer option may be wrong in one of several ways: It may misstate the facts of the question, it may misstate the law, it may misapply the law to the facts, or it may be under-inclusive or over-inclusive. If an answer is incorrect in any one respect (even if the other elements are correct), it is wrong. Eliminate it.

When you take a test like the Multistate Bar Exam, which is written by expert test-makers, you may be sure of one thing: There will almost certainly be no errors in the content or form of the questions. On an objective exam written by a law school professor, on the other hand, you may find an answer that is unintentionally under- or over-inclusive.

If the answers to a multiple choice question are written so that you simply can't tell with certainty which is the correct response, mark the answer you think is correct, but make sure you state your assumption in the margin of your answer sheet. You should do this even if you were told not to write anything other than the correct response. If there's a real defect in the test, you have one of two choices: 1) to form the best conclusion you can and select one of the options (which may or may not turn out to be correct) but write nothing to qualify your answer (this will create the risk of your being wrong even though you knew the law); or 2) to disregard your instructions and write in the margin to prove that you did indeed know the law. An objective test, like a subjective test, should be an accurate reflection of your knowledge. If a defect in the test prevents you from proving your knowledge, you shouldn't have to lose any points.

Watch for Traps

A professional test-maker will not try to trick you. He will test you only on your knowledge and analytical ability and will expect you to read his question unambiguously and to interpret it without reservations or qualifications. A non-professional test-maker, on the other hand, may sometimes be confused about the skills he is testing. Instead of testing your understanding of the law and your ability to analyze the issues, he may trip you up over inconsequential details and "tricky" issues. Say, for example, he has written a true/false question on a Constitutional Law exam that reads, "The 1952 case *Brown v. Board of Education* abolished the 'separate but equal' concept. . . ." Only the date is wrong—the *Brown* case was decided in 1954, not 1952. By burying the error in a subordinate clause, this professor is taking a cheap shot that may confuse you into picking the wrong answer option. This is not good exam-making. Nonetheless, if you find a question like this on an objective exam, watch out for more of them because you may have found the professor's *modus operandi.*

Guess Intelligently

On an objective exam, it's inevitable that you will be reduced to guessing on some answers. If you guess intelligently, however, you can dramatically increase the number of your correct answers. The following are some guidelines.

When to Guess

Don't guess until you've eliminated all the answers that are clearly wrong. Remember: If any element of an answer choice is wrong, it can't be the correct response.

In looking for incorrect answers, keep in mind that, to be correct, a response has to "fit" grammatically and logically with the question. For instance, if the question ends in "is . . . ," the answer should be in the singular, not plural. A small point like this may help you to rule out an incorrect answer.

Another way to eliminate incorrect responses is to "force" your memory of the subject raised by the question. As with memory blocks during essay exams, you should try to recall everything you possibly can about the topic (including any case that may have raised similar issues or dealt with similar facts). By doing this, you may find that you haven't really guessed at all but have "intuited" your way to the correct answer.

How to Guess

If you resort to simple guessing, you are just playing the odds. The answer you wind up with may not be correct, but you have at least a 25 percent chance of selecting the correct one (greater if you've already eliminated one or two obviously incorrect ones). In any event, you're more likely to choose the correct one if you keep the following tips in mind.

If Two Answers Are Exact Opposites, One of Them Is Probably the Correct Answer

This is a traditional feature of objective tests. When two answers are direct opposites, the professor is probably testing your ability to distinguish the correct rule from the incorrect one, so one of the two conflicting options is likely to be the correct one.

Stay Away from Absolutes

Answers containing words such as "always," "never," "none," "all," "must," or "only" should be viewed with suspicion. Obviously, these words permit no exceptions to the rule they are describing. Since there are few rules in the law with *no* exceptions, any statement that uses one or several of these words is more apt to be false than not.

By the same token, when an answer contains a qualifier such as "some," "often," "rarely," "may," "probably," "usually," "could," "might," and "sometimes," that answer is more likely to be true because it allows for exceptions.

Longer Statements Are More Likely to Be True Than Shorter Ones

It takes more qualifiers to make a statement true than it does to make one false. As a result, a longer statement is usually a better guess than a shorter one.

"All of the Above" Is Usually a Good Guess

Because it's easier to write true statements that sound plausible than write false statements, the answer "all of the above" is generally a good guess.

"None of the Above" Is Usually a Poor Guess

"None of the above" is a "non-answer." Since false answers are more difficult to conceive and write than true ones, "none of the above" is generally a poor guess.

If Two of Four Answers Are Virtually Identical, Pick the Longer of the Two

Usually, the longer answer includes an extra qualifier. Since qualifiers make an answer more likely to be correct, the longer of two very similar answers is more likely to be the correct one.

Choose the Answer That Has the Most Elements in Common with the Other Choices

One way a good test-maker "buries" a correct answer is to surround it with other choices that contain some elements of the truth but that omit at least one of the elements. The correct response, therefore, is likely to have a lot in common with the other responses. Look for the choice that has the greatest number of elements in common with the others but that has at least one additional, seemingly reasonable and logical element.

On a True/False Question, "True" Is More Likely to Be the Correct Response

Since it's easier to write a true statement than to create a false one that is plausible, true statements are likely to be correct more often than false ones.

Guesses Dictated by the Sequence of Answer Choices

Where an answer appears in the sequence of options often matters. Here are the general rules for taking sequence into account:

- ✔ Statistically, the first answer is the least likely to be correct. Non-professional test-makers generally place the correct answer further down the list.
- ✔ If most questions have four answer choices, but this one has five, pick the fifth answer.

✔ When all (or most) questions have five possible
answers, those most likely to be correct, statistically,
are B, C, or D.

Post-Test Advice

The day you've been waiting for has finally arrived: Your exams are over!
Here are a few additional pieces of advice.

It Doesn't Matter How You Feel Now About Your Performance

Most people feel worried and unsure of themselves after a first-year
law exam. But remember, it's all over and there's nothing more you
can do about it. Furthermore, there's absolutely no correlation
between your feelings of anxiety and your exam performance.

Don't Take Part in Postmortems, and Don't Hang Around When Other Students Do

All you can do by engaging in postmortems in to increase your anxiety. The more you think about your exams, the more you'll conclude
that you could have done better. In reality, you won't remember your
answers accurately and you have no accurate way of measuring your
performance against the performance of your fellow students, so the
whole process is silly and self-defeating. Remember—not all best
exams or "A" answers are alike. A student who spotted an issue that
you didn't see did not necessarily perform better overall than you did.
She may well have dreamed up an issue that wasn't there, or she may
have missed one or several issues that you saw clearly. You don't have
the tools to compare yourself with others—only your professor does.
So relax and turn your thoughts to your temporary freedom and to
other pleasures.

Most Important: Forget About Law School and Enjoy Your Break!

GOOD LUCK!!!

SAMPLE WEEKLY SCHEDULE

	MON	TUES	WED	THURS	FRI	SAT	SUN
7:00 to 9:00							
9:00 to 10:00							
10:00 to 11:00							
11:00 to 12:00							
12:00 to 2:00							
2:00 to 3:00							
3:00 to 5:00							
5:00 to 6:00							
6:00 to 7:30							
7:30 to 9:00							
9:00 to 11:00							

SAMPLE CASE BRIEF

Case Brief

Brief Number: _____   Date: _____

Course: _____

Case Information

Case name: _____

Court: _____

Plaintiff: _____

Defendant: _____

Other parties: _____

_____

Case Type (Select all that apply)

❑ Landmark case ❑ Statement of majority rule ❑ Statement of minority rule

❑ Historical case ❑ Important dissenting opinion ❑ Statement of older, superseded rule

❑ Bad decision ❑ Other: _____

Fact Pattern

Facts: _____

_____

_____

_____

_____

_____

_____

_____

Keywords: _____

Procedural History

Prior procedural history: _____

_____

_____

_____

Lower court decision: _____

This court's ruling: _____

Concise Rule of Law

Rule of case: _____

_____

_____

_____

_____

Issue #1   **Issue:** _____

_____

_____

Rule of law: _____

_____

Rationale (Application of law to facts): _____

_____

_____

_____

_____

_____

Issue #2
(if applicable)   **Issue:** _____

_____

_____

Rule of law: _____

_____

Rationale (Application of law to facts): _____

_____

_____

_____

_____

Issue #3
(if applicable)   **Issue:** _____

_____

_____

Rule of law: _____

_____

Rationale (Application of law to facts): _____

_____

_____

_____

_____

SAMPLE CORNELL NOTES

NAME:
CLASS:
DATE:

Questions/Main Ideas/ Hypotheticals:	Class Notes:

Summary and Black-Letter Law